The
Portrait Miniature
in England

THE
PORTRAIT MINIATURE
IN ENGLAND

Katherine Coombs

V&A Publications

For my goddaughter Sophie

First published by V&A Publications, 1998

V&A Publications
160 Brompton Road, London SW3 1HW

Designed by Bernard Higton

ISBN 1851772073

A catalogue record for this book is available from the British Library

Printed in Hong Kong

Note: Unless otherwise stated, the miniatures have been enlarged.

COVER ILLUSTRATIONS

Front: Nicholas Hiliard, *Self-Portrait*, 1577. Watercolour on vellum, dia. 41mm.
Back: Details from left to right, clockwise: Simon Benninck, *Self-Portrait*, 1558 (Plate 9);
Nicholas Hilliard, *Self-Portrait*, 1577; Nicholas Hilliard, *Young Man Against a
Flame Background*, undated (Plate 17).

Frontispiece: Richard Cosway, *Arthur Wellesley*, later 1st Duke of Wellington, 1808.
Watercolour on ivory (71 x 56 mm). P.6-1941

CONTENTS

ACKNOWLEDGEMENTS

The wide scope but modest size of this book inevitably means that I owe a huge debt of gratitude to many writers, working not just in the field of miniatures but in related subjects from art clubs to academies to the City of London. I have indicated where possible those articles and books to which I have referred specifically and generally, and I hope this will allow the interested reader to return to the source of original investigations and ideas.

Anyone familiar with the study of miniature painting will recognise how indebted I am to many former curators at the Victoria and Albert Museum. I would particularly like to mention Graham Reynolds and Sir Roy Strong, both of whom have done so much to increase our knowledge of, and interest in, this subject.

It would be impossible to thank directly the many colleagues who have contributed over the years their knowledge about subjects that touch on miniatures and their settings, such as jewellery, snuff boxes, ivory carving, and many others. But I am able to thank those whose own researches in the field of miniature painting have led to many useful debates: Alan Derbyshire, Stephen Lloyd, Catharine MacLeod, John Murdoch and Vanessa Remington. For their help and support over the years, as well as in the preparation of this book, I would like to thank Malcolm Baker, Stephen Calloway, Kevin Edge, Sharon Fermor, Susan Lambert, Lionel Lambourne and Ronald Parkinson. Also Moira Thunder and my colleagues in the V&A Photographic Studio deserve particular mention for the photographs which have contributed so much to the appearance of this book.

I am particularly grateful to John Murdoch, former Keeper of the Department of Prints and Drawings at the V&A, who first gave me the opportunity to work in this field; to the V&A Research Department in which I found the necessary peace and quiet to write this book, and to V&A Publications, especially Clare Richards who helped me through the last stages with great patience and a clear eye.

Above all, I would like to pay tribute to the late V.J. Murrell (Jim) of the Conservation Department at the V&A. It was Jim who, with his sensitive and patient examination of the objects and his scholarly reading of the often misleading treatises of artists themselves, did so much to advance the study of this subject. Jim's approach was never that of the cold anatomist breaking down a painting to its constituent parts. It was he who first opened my eyes to the beauty of miniatures, who showed me that, despite their size and their often uncertain place in the 'History of Art', they reward close attention and consideration.

INTRODUCTION

Plate 1. Louis Nicholas van Blarenberghe, attributed to, 10 paintings set in the lid, bottom and sides of a gold octagonal snuff-box (Paris 1764-86), 1764. Watercolour on vellum. On the Continent small genre scenes and landscapes in miniature were popular. These reveal, more than the portraiture favoured in England, the roots of miniatures in book illumination. 922-1882

What is a Miniature?

Limning, a thing apart … which excelleth all other painting whatsoever.

NICHOLAS HILLIARD, *THE ART OF LIMNING* (C.1598)

This well-known observation by perhaps the most famous miniaturist, Nicholas Hilliard (*c.*1547–1619), emphasises two important points about the art of miniature painting: that in England what today are called miniatures were originally called limnings, and that limning was distinct and separate from other types of painting. Contrary to popular belief, miniature paintings are not simply small variants of oil paintings. The word 'miniature' comes from the Latin *miniare*, meaning to colour with red lead, originally related to book production before the invention of printing. In England the small, bright illustrations of such sacred books, painted in watercolour on vellum, were more usually called illuminations or limnings. Both terms derive from the medieval Latin word *luminare*, meaning to give light. In

1598 Richard Haydocke wrote 'Illuminating or limning, the perfection of painting...This was much used in former times in churchbookes (as is well known)'.[1] At the same time Nicholas Hilliard wrote *The Art of Limning*, describing the use of limning for painting portraits. A few decades later Edward Norgate's treatise *Miniatura – or the Art of Limning* used the Italian for illumination, *miniatura,* in the same context as the English word limning.[2] It was not long before 'miniature' came to express all things small, by association with the size of many limnings and a misleading link to words incorporating the Latin *min*, expressing smallness, such as 'minor'.

The Portrait Miniature in England

Another common misconception about miniature painting is that it was a peculiarly English practice. This is partly because many writers have devoted themselves to the study of English portrait miniatures; however, there were many artists across Europe who worked in this medium. Indeed, the first English portrait miniatures painted at the court of Henry VIII (r.1509–47) were almost certainly by an artist from the city of Ghent, in what is now Belgium. The first two notable practitioners of the portrait miniature were the German Hans Holbein (1497/8–1543), who worked for Henry VIII, and François Clouet (1516–72), who worked for the French court (Plate 2).

While the development of the portrait miniature can be traced through four hundred years of English history, elsewhere in Europe the art was not sustained to the same degree. After François Clouet's death in 1572 no artist of the same calibre took his place, although limnings continued to be painted in France. Meanwhile in England, during the same year that Clouet died, the twenty-five-year-old Nicholas Hilliard had his first sitting with Queen Elizabeth I (r.1558–1603) and embarked on a productive career lasting over 40 years. Hilliard established limning as a leading and separate art and secured a place for miniatures at the heart of Elizabethan culture.

One possible reason for the very different histories of limning in England and on the Continent is suggested by the backgrounds of its practitioners. Clouet, and indeed Holbein, were primarily trained as oil painters. Both probably first sketched portraits in chalk on paper – many such drawings survive today – and from these sketches then painted versions either in oil or in miniature. For these two artists miniatures were just another form of painting and did not dominate their working lives. In contrast, Hilliard was trained as a goldsmith rather than a painter. Painting in England at this time was regarded as a mechanical art, in Hilliard's words 'for furnishing of houses...for tapestries, or building, or any other work'. For Hilliard limning was 'a thing apart from all other painting' and 'tendeth not to common men's use'. While Hilliard worked in other media, such as printing, he identified himself primarily as a limner and established an awareness of limning and its practitioners as separate and unique. In 1584 a draft monopoly for manufacturing portraits proposed that George Gower, the Serjeant-Painter in the Queen's Household, should have a monopoly of 'all manner of portraits and pictures' of the queen, 'excepting only one Nicholas Hilliard' who was to have the right 'to make portraits...of our body and person in small compass in limning only'. Although there is no evidence that this was enacted, in 1599 Hilliard was granted an annuity of £40 by Elizabeth in which he was described as a goldsmith and 'our limner'. James I (r.1603–25) inherited Hilliard as 'limner' to the

monarch, and Hilliard's son Laurence (?1581–p.1640) was to succeed to this position on his father's death.

It is arguable that Hilliard's success, in the last two decades of Elizabeth's reign, was due to England's detachment from Europe in the 1580s; after the Pope's excommunication of Elizabeth encouraged Catholic Spain to threaten invasion. On the Continent portrait limning was one of a number of subjects and styles available to artists and patrons. However, in England, Protestant suspicion of religious imagery both encouraged portraiture and limited the awareness of Continental art. By the reign of Charles I (1625–49), such insularity began to give way. The connoisseur king and a number of his aristocratic friends built up collections of Italian and Netherlandish paintings. In 1629 Charles commissioned Sir Peter Paul Rubens (1577–1640) to paint the ceiling of the Banqueting House in Whitehall and in 1632 invited Rubens' pupil, Sir Anthony Van Dyck (1599–1641), to England, who revolutionised the appearance of portraiture in England.

Through all these developments the miniature portrait not only survived but flourished. Both patrons and artists continued to commission and practise this distinct art. John Hoskins (c.1595–1665) took on the mantle of Hilliard; and Sir Kenelm Digby famously noted that 'the best faces are seldom satisfied with Van Dyck; whereas not the very worst even complained of Hoskins'[4], indicating that miniatures appealed to their patrons in a distinct way from oils. Van Dyck's reputation neither obliterated the name of Hoskins nor forced miniature portraiture into the margins. Hoskins' nephew, Samuel Cooper (1609–72), specifically trained and practised as a limner and became the most internationally renowned English artist of his day.

Another factor possibly accounting for the different profiles of English and Continental limning is that there has been little discussion of miniature as a separate art on the Continent. This is significant as our understanding of the art of the past is influenced by what was valued and encouraged at the time, and by what has been preserved and recorded in later years. Hilliard himself, writing in 1598 about his artistic influences, recorded the name of only one limner from earlier years: Hans Holbein. However, for 30 years, between Holbein's death and Hilliard's first portrait of Queen Elizabeth, other limners were painting portrait miniatures, and it is they who kept the art alive and must have indicated to Hilliard, a goldsmith, the potential market for these watercolour paintings. As Hilliard chose not to mention them by name they vanished from the picture.

On the Continent, the reputations of a few artists such as François Clouet and Giulio Clovio (1498–1578) have survived. Their very different uses of limning, however, mean that they are not studied together. Clouet was a great portraitist, and his miniatures are invariably discussed as part of his wider practice or as a footnote in works on French portraiture. Clovio, working in Italy, continued the tradition of limning religious works and is usually discussed within the field of illuminated manuscripts.

This is strikingly different from the situation in England, where there was not only a tradition of minia-ture painting but, perhaps more significantly, an estab-lished interest in limning as a separate practice. In 1598, Richard Haydocke's English translation of Giovanni Paolo Lomazzo's *Trattato,* 'a tracte containing the Artes of Curious paintinge…' was published. Haydocke admired Giorgio Vasari for preserving the names of Italian artists in his *Lives of the Most Excellent Painters, Sculptors and Architects* (*c.*1550) and wished that an English equivalent existed: 'Then would Mr Nicholas Hilliard's hand [and] ingenious Illuminating or Limming, the perfection of painting' be compared with the art of Italians such as Raphael. Indeed it seems that it

Plate 2. François Clouet, attributed to *Catherine de Medicis, c.*1555. Watercolour on vellum (60 x 44 mm). Miniature painting was not confined to England, and this beautiful miniature confirms Clouet's reputation as one of the great miniature painters. P.26-1954

Figure 1. Cabinet, designed by Horace Walpole probably in collaboration with William Kent, 1743. Kingwood with ivory (152 x 91 x 22 cm). In a letter of 1743 Walpole wrote of his 'new cabinet for my enamels and miniatures', including works by Hans Holbein and Isaac Oliver, which formed the centrepiece of a room devoted to art. W.52-1925

was Haydocke who persuaded Hilliard to write about limning. Hilliard's treatise was not published at the time but hand-written copies circulated among interested professionals and amateurs, and quotations appeared in a number of later published works such as William Sanderson's *Graphice, The Use of the Pen and Pensil* (1658), Alexander Browne's *Ars Pictoria* (1669 and 1675), and William Salmon's *Polygraphice* (1672). These works often pay tribute to limners, thereby preserving their names and their contribution to limning as Haydocke had hoped.

By the end of the seventeenth century, limning was already viewed in retrospect as a distinct element of English artistic life. John Dryden's translation of Charles du Fresnoy's *Art of Painting* (1695) was published with 'A short Account of the most Eminent painters, both ancient and Modern' by Richard Graham.[5] Included with biographies of Continental artists such as Leonardo da Vinci, Albrecht Dürer, and Giulio Clovio was the earliest biography of Samuel Cooper (?1608–1672) 'the most excellent Limner in his Time', who had died only 20 years before. Interestingly, Graham noted how difficult it had been to find information about English masters compared to even minor artists on the Continent. More significantly, an English translation of Roger de Piles' *Art of Painting* (1706) had an additional chapter by Bainbrigge Buckeridge called 'Towards an English School' in which he defiantly sought to 'prove that the English Painter and Paintings, both for their Number and their Merit, have a better claim to the Title of a School, than those of France'; he also included biographies of Nicholas Hilliard, Isaac Oliver, John Hoskins, Richard Gibson, Thomas Flatman, Alexander and Samuel Cooper.[6]

These translations, read alongside texts about English artists, demonstrate the increasing awareness in the late seventeenth century of English art in a European context. Buckeridge noted of Cooper that he 'was a Performer in Miniature, of whom our nation can never sufficiently boast...and even equall'd the most famous Italians'. Increasingly, however, the intellectual climate cast the art of the Continent in a dominant role, and the art of England in a marginal and provincial one. The appreciation of the miniature in England became less aesthetically confident and increasingly bound up with an antiquarian interest in English history, the characters that peopled it and their portraits.

While the motive for interest in limnings had subtly

Figure 2. M. Gauci, facsimile of a self-portrait by George Vertue, the printmaker and antiquarian. Vertue is seen here holding a miniature of his patron, Edward Harley, the great miniature collector. E.2229-1889

changed, it nonetheless ensured their continuing role in English culture. The antiquarian and printmaker George Vertue (1709–56) took a leading role in disseminating images of limnings to a wider audience and also collected information about the artists (fig. 2).[7] Great historical collections of miniatures also began to be brought together, such as that of Vertue's patron Edward Harley, that of Dr Mead who owned the limning *Head of Christ* by Isaac Oliver (c.1560–1617) (Plate 3), and that of Horace Walpole (fig. 1), the son of the Prime Minister, Robert Walpole. When Vertue died Horace Walpole bought his notes and rewrote and published them in five volumes, the last in 1770. Interestingly, he called his volumes *Anecdotes of Painting in England*, rather than a history, and with revealing mock modesty

Plate 3. Isaac Oliver, *Head of Christ* (signed), c.1615. Watercolour on vellum (53 x 43 mm). This miniature was in the collection of the famous 18th-century collector Dr Richard Mead, and was particularly admired for the soft-focus effect of its extraordinary stipple technique. P15-1931

described them as 'trifling', the painters as 'insignificant', and the material as 'scarce worth arranging'.

While past limnings were subjected to the judgement of a new age, miniature painting continued to be practised throughout the eighteenth and nineteenth centuries in Britain. When the Royal Academy was founded in 1768 to nurture a British School, miniatures were placed at the heart of the main exhibition room (fig. 14). On the Continent, especially in France, miniature painting achieved a similar level of prominence and popularity. This renaissance has since attracted the interest of collectors and writers. However, Continental miniatures of this period were quite distinct from English miniatures (Plate 3) and there was limited exchange of ideas and influence across the Channel; consequently the two have invariably been treated separately.

The portrait miniature continued to be popular until it

was dealt a body blow by the invention of photography in the middle of the nineteenth century. In 1857, at the same time as the detrimental effect of photography on miniature painting began to be noticed, the South Kensington Museum (re-named the Victoria and Albert Museum in 1899) was established. It had no brief to collect miniatures and indeed the first example acquired by the museum in 1857 was purchased by the enamel department for its wonderful locket (Plate 31). The first issue of the catalogue *Pictures, Drawings and Etchings* (1859) contained no miniatures but commented in the section on watercolours that 'From the earliest time there was one branch of art in which English artists had a reputation even on the continent, and in which they certainly excelled the artists of other nations, namely miniature painting in water-colours'. In 1862 'antiquarian' miniatures by such artists as Hilliard and Oliver figured prominently in a huge loan exhibition. As the Director noted, these miniatures 'were objects of so much interest' that a further exhibition was planned of 'this art in which English artists were the first to excel, and which, though now seldom practised, flourished in England for nearly three centuries'.[8] This 1865 exhibition of nearly 4000 miniatures, borrowed from private collections, provided a survey from the miniature's beginnings to its apparent demise only a decade earlier. These exhibitions were the first time that the public had seen the work of artists such as Hilliard and Cooper, which had been cherished for centuries in private family collections. The exhibition cast the Museum in the role of promoter and protector of this art, thereby attracting gifts of miniatures.

In 1908 a government committee on museums noted that no institution 'collected' miniatures – although all 'haphazardly' acquired them – and argued that miniatures had 'no relation to the applied art', which was the brief of the V&A, and consequently no place there. Perhaps defiantly, the V&A immediately published the first miniatures catalogue. Two years later a significant collection of miniatures belonging to the late George Salting was offered to the nation, which the V&A succeeded in acquiring. Including such now famous miniatures as Hilliard's *Young Man Among Roses* (Plate 18) this established the V&A as the focus for collecting and research, led by such notable curators as Basil Long. Additionally, as the home of the National Watercolour Collection, the V&A situated miniature painting as an English watercolour art, precursor and integral part of the 'English tradition' of watercolour painting.

CHAPTER ONE

THE ORIGINS AND DEVELOPMENT OF THE PORTRAIT MINIATURE

[Limning] excelleth all other painting whatsoever in sundry points...being fittest for the decking of princes' bookes...for the imitation of the purest flowers and most beautiful creatures in the finest and purest colours...and is for the service of noble persons very meet, in small volumes, in private manner, for them to have the portraits and pictures of themselves, their peers, or any other foreign persons which are of interest to them.

NICHOLAS HILLIARD, THE ART OF LIMNING (C.1598)

Limning, watercolour painting, was the subject of the first book on painting published in English: an anonymous work known today simply as *Limning* (1573). This, however, was concerned solely with the decoration of books. In contrast, Nicholas Hilliard's treatise *The Art of Limning* was concerned with the limning of portraits, 'in small volumes', 'in private manner': what we today would describe as portrait miniatures. Hilliard was an innovative artist who raised the profile of the miniature portrait to a level where Shakespeare used them as plot devices in his plays and John Donne wrote a poem praising Hilliard's work: 'A hand or an eye by Hilliard is worth an history by a worse painter'.[1] And yet Hilliard was not the originator of this art. The earliest surviving English portrait miniature is of Henry VIII, painted around 1526, nearly half a century before Elizabeth first sat to Hilliard (Plate 4).

Miniatures at the Court of Henry VIII

To imagine the impact of the first miniature portrait at the court of Henry VIII, one has to imagine an entirely different visual world from that of today in which we are swamped by endless printed images. The printing press was only introduced in England in 1483 and early English printed illustrations were rare and very crude compared to their Continental counterparts. When

Henry VIII came to the throne in 1509 easel painting was equally rare and unsophisticated. Occasional portraits were required by royalty, usually during marriage negotiations, but on the whole these were far from our idea of an individual likeness. Although the monarch's image appeared on official documents it was more like the image of a king on a playing-card than of a recognisable individual. Portraiture, for the most part, was confined to tomb sculpture for the very wealthy, while graphic arts, namely painting, drawing and printing, did not have the prominent role they were to have in later years.

But it would be wrong to assume that this was an artistically impoverished era. At the end of Henry VIII's reign an inventory of the late king's goods listed a staggering number of precious objects: the contents of endless rooms, coffers and cabinets, revealing the visually rich world created by this flamboyant and profligate king.[2] Painting did have a place at Henry's court but, like all sixteenth-century monarchs, Henry VIII employed his 'painters' for temporary work intended to create a spectacular visual environment such as decorating palaces, barges and furniture; painting heraldic banners for grand ceremonies; and providing sets for elaborate court entertainments in which the king and his courtiers often took part.

The Serjeant Painter, whose task it was to organise such projects, was also responsible for the continued demand for portraits. The king also received portraits as gifts from foreign courts, creating a sizeable gallery of paintings, most of which were carefully covered with yellow and white 'sarsonet curtaiins'. This meant that each work had to be viewed individually rather than being treated decoratively en masse. It was the subject matter of paintings, whether the image of Christ or of an esteemed prince, which rendered these objects precious. This would have been particularly true of the earliest

portrait miniatures, all of which were of the king's most intimate circle.

The earliest miniatures are small in number, and compared to the miniatures of Hilliard they seem almost naive. But they were made to be held in the hand and they reward the close attention for which they were designed. The *Henry VIII* in the Fitzwilliam Museum (Plate 4) shows him before the onset of bloated middle age. The other portraits include the first of his six wives, Katherine of Aragon (in one she is holding a small monkey), their daughter Mary, and of the longed-for son and heir, Edward VI, as a child. Attempts to identify the portraits of other court ladies, based on the date of their costume and by matching their jewels with descriptions in surviving inventories of the Royal Wardrobe and Jewel House have not proved conclusive. None of these miniatures are signed and a number date from after the arrival of Hans Holbein at Henry's court in 1536. Holbein also did not sign his work, and while a number of his miniatures are well-documented, such as *Anne of Cleves* (Plate 6), other possible miniatures by Holbein have to be distinguished from other unsigned works dating from 1536 onwards.

The Attribution of Early Miniatures

At a time when most artists did not sign their work, their names and reputations come down to us through written sources. To identify the miniature painter working for Henry VIII before Holbein's arrival, we have to scour all the documents of the time for the name of a likely candidate whose dates roughly fit those of the miniatures. As many miniatures as possible from the period are then gathered together – not an easy task since they are scattered throughout different collections and countries. Attempts to identify the work of separate artists are made by grouping miniatures sharing similar style and techniques; 'style' is assessed by comparing the way each portrait is created, to develop a sense of what the works have in common, such as how the artist paints the background, the jewels, the way an eye is formed with a flick

Plate 4. Lucas Hornebolte, attributed to, *Henry VIII*, c.1524–6. Watercolour on vellum (53 x 48 mm). This miniature portrays the king in his mid-thirties; in other versions he is shown with the beard that he grew in competition with Francis I of France (fig. 5). This miniature is the lynch-pin of arguments identifying Lucas Hornebolte as the first painter of miniatures in England. (Fitzwilliam Museum, Cambridge. PD.19-1949)

of red in the corner, or a line around the iris. If shared characteristics emerge, the 'handwriting' of one artist can be identified. In this way an 'oeuvre' is created, against which all later attributions will be compared. This is what happened with Lucas Horenbout (now frequently known by the anglicised version of his name Hornebolte) and the miniatures dating from the early part of Henry VIII's reign.

In 1948 the Fitzwilliam *Henry VIII* (Plate 4) was tentatively attributed to Lucas Hornebolte.[3] A first clue was an early account of Hans Holbein, written in 1604 stating that Holbein was taught limning by 'Master Lucas'.[4] As more evidence about an artist called Lucas Hornebolte was gleaned from various documents, the possibility that 'Master Lucas' was Hornebolte suggested itself. In 1959 the first payment to Lucas Hornebolte by Henry VIII was discovered in Henry's Chamber accounts for September 1525.[5] The Fitzwilliam *Henry VIII* is inscribed 'anno XXXV', and although it is not clear how precisely to interpret 'year 35' (Henry could be in his 35th year or aged 35) it narrows the date of the miniature to between June 1524, Henry's 34th birthday and June 1526, his 36th birthday. The coincidence between the appearance of both an artist called 'Lucas' at court and the first-known miniature portrait seemed suggestive. Once the painting was given to Hornebolte, it was possible to group other miniatures from the same period around it and attribute them to Hornebolte.[6]

Although Lucas Hornebolte is not now as shrouded in mystery, the interpretation of the documentary evidence is open to argument. Lucas, his father Gerard and his sister Susannah, were all artists from Ghent who came to live in England around 1525. It is not proven, however, that the Horneboltes specifically came to work as book limners, and so the nature and extent of Lucas Hornebolte's work for Henry remains unclear.[7] In Ghent, Gerard was a master painter who ran a workshop producing a wide variety of work. His name appears regularly in the accounts of Margaret of Austria for limnings for a Book of Hours, probably the famous Sforza Hours, now in the British Library. And yet since Gerard ran a workshop he may not have personally carried out such limnings. There are no records of his son Lucas before he came to England, so nothing is known of his training. In Henry's accounts Lucas is described as a 'pictor maker' rather than a limner, in contrast to another artist, Richard James, clearly described as a 'lymner of bookes'. But while some doubt has been cast

Figure 3. Anonymous Flemish artist, 15th century, from a Book of Hours showing the Crucifixion. Watercolour on vellum. The angels in this decorative border are painted using identical techniques to the first English portrait miniature (Plate 4). The angels are painted in gold over brown ochre against a background of red pigment (vermilion). (British Library. MS.Add.35314)

the book illuminations of what we call the 'Ghent-Bruges School', shorthand for illuminators working in these two Flemish cities whose work shared distinct and unique characteristics.[8] Technical analysis and comparison between manuscripts from the Ghent-Bruges School and miniatures attributed to Hornebolte have shown more clearly how the two are related.[9]

The decorated border of the Fitzwilliam *Henry VIII* (Plate 4) suggests that the artist was probably trained in book illustration. The portrait is painted within a circle, but the miniature is rectangular like a page from a small book with stylised angels in the corners. Not only is this motif found in numerous border decorations of books painted by the Ghent-Bruges School, but more importantly the angels are painted using identical techniques (fig. 3).

Similarly the treatment of the flesh is related to Ghent-Bruges techniques. In the area of the face the artist laid a smooth and opaque layer of paint with a hint of flesh colour, later called the 'carnation'. Hornebolte's carnations are usually a warm pink hue and the features modelled with tiny, short lines (hatches) of transparent red and grey.

The smooth, brilliant blue backgrounds Hornebolte used in his miniatures also had their counterparts in Flemish book decoration and became a hallmark of miniatures until the end of Hilliard's career. The technique for painting gold jewellery had its origins in the trompe-l'oeil jewels in many late fifteenth-century Flemish manuscripts, intended to deceive the eye into thinking the page was adorned with jewels. These jewels, like the angels, are painted in dark ochre with gold paint to bring out the detail.

on much of the certainty that was hardening around the name of 'Lucas Hornebolte', on balance the family's involvement with limning cannot be denied. When Albrecht Dürer met Gerard in Antwerp in May 1521, he described him as an 'illuminator' and bought from Susannah an illumination of Christ, praising her highly for her work.

The Technical Influence of the Ghent-Bruges School

Even if we cannot assume that Hornebolte came to England specifically to run a workshop dedicated to the limning of books, the miniature portraits themselves show definite links with the technical and stylistic practices of the workshops of Ghent in which Hornebolte's father was a major practitioner, and within which Lucas was probably trained. Similarities have been found between the miniature portraits painted in England and

Possible Origins of the Separate Miniature Portrait

For centuries limning was practised within the great monastic institutions to produce precious hand-painted books. However, by the late middle ages wealthy patrons commissioned such texts for their own private chapels,

Plate 5. Anonymous Flemish artist, detail of the decorative border from a Book of Hours showing a pendant containing a miniature of Christ, 15th century. Watercolour on vellum. This illumination indicates that the use of limning to create small images in a jewel-like setting possibly originated with small devotional images rather than portraits.
(British Library. MS. Add.18852)

or as a gift to a religious institution. These texts often included a 'portrait' of the patron praying or donating the book to an institution's patron saint. Limning moved from the confines of religious institutions as demand led to the creation of independent workshops.

The separation of limning from books seems to have occurred in response both to the development of the printing press, which made hand-written books increasingly redundant except as luxury objects, and to competition with the workshops of panel painters. Limners increasingly competed for patronage with the painters of independent paintings, producing separate

limnings to be hung on the wall for devotional or decorative purposes. Another possible use for the separate devotional limning, similar in its jewel-like setting to the later portrait miniature, is suggested by the illustration of a pendant containing an image of Christ (Plate 5).[10] No such portrait-like images of saints set in this way survive today, but there are pendants from Spain and Italy with limned religious scenes protected under slivers of rock crystal (a form of quartz), which when cut thinly is very like glass.

Three other portrait traditions could have suggested the portrait miniature, all alluding to classical traditions of portraiture: the metal coin set with the emperor's, or monarch's, head; the classical medal cast in relief out of metal; and the classical cameo also carved in relief but out of precious stone. Medals were often heavy and large, and were displayed in a cabinet rather than worn. The cameo was smaller and more jewel-like and would have suggested the desirability of portraiture on this

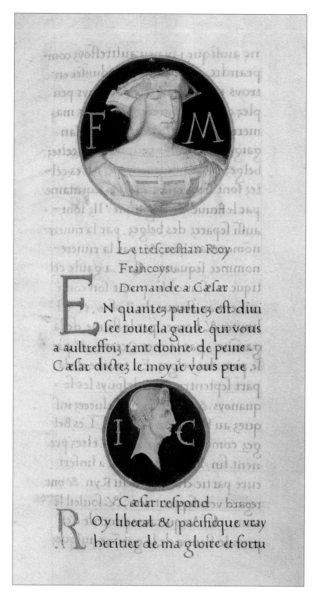

Figure 4. Page from *Les Commentaires de la Guerre Gallique*, Volume I, 1519. Illuminated manuscript on vellum (250 x 125 mm). One of three volumes ordered by Louise of Savoy for her son Francis I of France. This page juxtaposes portraits of Francis and Julius Caesar reminiscent of classical models, the medal and the cameo profile, a comparison intended to flatter Francis.
(British Library. Harley MS 6205)

scale. Limners would often mimic these types, faithfully imitating the monochrome of metal or stone. A page from the first volume of a text called the *Guerre de Gallique* (fig. 4) is an interesting halfway point to the portrait miniature: two heads relate to medal and cameo

types but have been left as drawings rather than mimicking the colour of stone or metal. These are set against a blue background, edged with gold, much as later miniatures would be. In the following volume another limner takes the next logical step, effectively colouring in such portraits using a naturalistic colour range. Here, the limner has not imitated another form of portraiture, the medal or cameo, but has effectively created a new type of limned portrait which would seem like the later portrait miniature if cut from the page.[11]

On 2 December 1526 the secretary to the Venetian ambassador in England wrote to his brother about two unusual gifts Henry VIII had received from the sister of Francis I. These seem to have been a form of locket, a tiny case with a gold cover attached on one side which opened to reveal a portrait of Francis I 'very naturally painted'.[12] The other was also in gold and opened in the same way but contained two portraits, one of the Dauphin, heir to the French throne, and his brother Henry. The children were hostages of Emperor Charles V to ensure payment of the ransom for Francis I who had been captured in battle. These novel images were intended to elicit support for their plight.

These two miniatures are not known today, although a miniature of the Dauphin in the Royal Collection is possibly a copy. But it is assumed that they were painted by the same artist who painted the portraits in Volume Two of the *Guerre de Gallique*, which have been attributed to Jean Clouet. Jean Clouet, like Lucas Hornebolte, was effectively forgotten for centuries. As Hornebolte was eclipsed by Holbein, so Jean Clouet was eclipsed by his famous son François (Plate 1). Unsurprisingly, the history of Jean Clouet and the attribution of works to him has provoked as much controversy as that surrounding Hornebolte. It has emerged, however, that Jean Clouet was not French but was classed as a 'foreigner' in France, and like Hornebolte was probably from the Low Countries.[13] It has been suggested that either Hornebolte saw the miniatures by his fellow countryman and copied the idea, or that the king was amused by these gifts and directed Hornebolte to follow this lead from the court of Francis I. Thus, Clouet has been credited with the innovation of the portrait miniature. However, as has been demonstrated, the impulse to create a separate portrait miniature came from a variety of sources. Too much evidence has been lost for the portrait miniature ever to be classed as the innovation of one country or individual.

Figure 5. Letters Patent of 1524, with a portrait of Henry VIII attributed to Lucas Hornebolte. Vellum. This is an early example of a version of a miniature portrait (Plate 4) that was used on official documents. A letters patent, by which the king conferred property or position on a subject, often carried an image of the monarch.
(Private collection – on loan to the V&A)

Possible Settings and Uses of Early Portrait Miniatures

Most early miniatures are clearly in later settings, but it has been suggested that the simple round turned ivory cases with 'cristall' covers described in the inventories of Charles I were the original settings.[14] At this date ivory turning was certainly practised in England, although general glass-making was too unsophisticated for such delicate glass covers. However, these might either literally have been slivers of rock crystal or, if glass, could have been provided by spectacle makers; the Venetian ambassador described the miniatures sent to Henry VIII from France as resembling the 'spechi da fuoco' sold in St Mark's Square (burning glasses to raise fire from the sun), which hints at this possibility.[15] The assumption, however, that all English miniatures at this date were set in round ivory cases ignores other evidence. Two of the earliest miniatures, the *Henry VIII* (Plate 4) and one of Katherine of Aragon holding a monkey (private collection), are rectangular and would have required a different setting. It has been suggested that these could have been cut at a later date from a manuscript, but comparing the quality of painting in the *Henry VIII* with

a version of it used in a letters patent (fig. 5), the former appears more finished and seems to have been intended to be set separately and viewed closely rather than subordinate to a text.

The year after Henry VIII received the gift from France, he returned two miniatures, of himself and of his daughter, Mary. Bearing in mind the symbolic and even mystical qualities attributed to jewels at this time, and the competition with the French court, Henry would have ensured that the settings were magnificent. An indication of how magnificent is found in the inventory of goods taken after his death in 1547. In the Queen's Jewel House a personal coffer contained 'a tablet of golde having on thone side the Kinges Picture peynted and on thesone side is a roose of Dyamountes and Rubies', surrounded by more diamonds, rubies and an emerald.

It seems likely that this 'peynted' picture of the king was a limning, since the accounts of Henry VIII's last queen, Catherine Parr, record a payment in 1547 to 'Lucas wyfe for makynge of the Queenes pykture and the Kynges' which could be money owed to Hornebolte's widow for work he had done.[16] A letter of 17 May 1547 from Lord Seymour to the widowed queen, soon to be his wife, also indicates her fondness of such small

Opposite: Plate 6. Hans Holbein, *Anne of Cleves*, 1539. Watercolour on vellum (dia. 44.5 mm), with turned ivory lid. It is still possible to screw the rose lid to its base; this perfect fit seems to be the result of both having been carved from one piece of elephant tusk.
P.153-1910

Plate 7. Lucas Hornebolte, *The Emperor Charles V*, c.1525. Watercolour on vellum (dia. 42 mm). Charles V was the nephew of Catherine of Aragon and undoubtedly made her a gift of his portrait. The oil, of which this portrait is a copy, was listed in Henry VIII's 1542 inventory and is still in the Royal Collection today.
P.22-1942

portraits: 'Also I shall humbely desyer yor highnesse to give me one of your small pictures, if ye have any left'.[17]

Sadly Henry VIII's inventory neither confirms nor disproves the suggestion that miniatures were set in ivory cases. There are vague references such as 'little cofer of cipresse with viii Boxes with phisionomyes', but, for example, no record of the clearly beautiful ivory case for *Anne of Cleves* (Plate 6). This probably is contemporary but it is perhaps significant that while such skilled turning was common on the Continent, particularly in Germany, no other boxes like this are known today, except one other in England containing the Parker jewel, but dating from 50 years later (on loan to the V&A). It is possible that Holbein arranged for this to be specially made while he was in Augsberg, Germany, painting *Anne of Cleves*.

This fragmentary evidence seems to suggest that a miniature intended as a gift would have been magnificently set, while the 'phisionomes', possibly copies of oils (see Plate 7), were kept in simple boxes. Henry VIII does not seem to have had a special coffer or cabinet for his miniatures, and the many 'phisionomes' in boxes were scattered among various coffers. However, as the Scottish ambassador witnessed in 1564, Elizabeth I, who must have inherited her father's miniatures, carefully kept them in a cabinet in her most private room.[18]

Lucas Hornebolte and Hans Holbein at the Court of Henry VIII

The portrait miniature clearly became an established art within court circles, since Holbein felt it advisable to learn the art himself. Today Holbein is seen primarily as a portrait painter, but the variety of his work is surprising, from making a cradle for Princess Elizabeth to painting a huge dynastic wall-painting of Henry VIII in Whitehall Palace, as well as designing for jewellers and goldsmiths, and supplying printers with book illustrations.

These two foreign artists had very different approaches to their working lives in England. In 1534 Hornebolte received a formal grant of the office of King's painter and on the same day became a denizen, a special form of citizenship granted to foreigners, allowing him to employ four journeymen (qualified workmen approved by the guilds). These journeymen could have provided

Plate 8. Hans Holbein, *Mrs Jane Small*, formerly known as a portrait of Mrs Robert Pemberton, *c.*1540. Watercolour on vellum (dia. 52 mm), later frame. The wife of a rich London merchant, Jane Small lived in the same parish as the steelyard merchants Holbein had painted before he was employed by the king. P.40-1935

repetitions of Hornebolte's work such as the version of Henry VIII set in a letters patent (fig. 5). Questions of originality were of little concern to artists at this date and while Hornebolte clearly painted miniatures from life, two copies of oils, one of Charles V (Plate 7) and the other of Margaret Beaufort, grandmother of Henry VIII, were possibly part of a wider brief to provide miniature versions of dynastically important portraits for the king.[19]

Holbein never painted such copies and was given prestigious commissions such as the king's prospective wives (Plate 6), but Hornebolte does not seem to have suffered in terms of the king's personal favour. In 1544 the royal patent confirming Hornebolte as King's painter paid tribute to the 'science and experience in the pictorial art of Lucas Hornebolte' with which the king had long been personally acquainted. Nor did Hornebolte suffer financially – both men received salaries from the court equivalent to 55 shillings a month. There is even some evidence that Hornebolte admired Holbein's work; a copy of Holbein's self-portrait is generally attributed to Hornebolte, as are other copies after Holbein.

In contrast to Hornebolte, Holbein seems to have chosen a position of relative detachment and independence from the court. He never became a denizen, and kept his house in Basle ensuring that he could return if he wished. It has been observed that Holbein's quarterly payments set him apart from the retainers who closely attended the king, such as his musicians and falconers and indeed Hornebolte, who were all paid monthly.[20] Hornebolte seems to have worked exclusively for the king and the court, whereas Holbein, despite the high profile of his work for Henry, retained his independent portrait practice. One beautiful miniature by Holbein belies the reputation of the miniature as an exclusively court art (Plate 8). A coat of arms painted on a piece of vellum long-associated with this portrait identified the woman as Mrs Pemberton – always something of a puzzle since she was the wife of an obscure country gentleman from a Northamptonshire village, far from both the court and Holbein's practice in London. Recently, however, the evidence has been reinterpreted and the more likely explanation is that she was Mrs Jane Small, whose maiden name was Pemberton and who was the wife of a prosperous London merchant, Nicholas Small.[21]

Figure 6. Backs of two miniatures showing the playing-card support. The vellum was stuck to a playing-card for extra support, and a smooth join ensured by burnishing the back using a large canine tooth set in a wooden stick (fig. 9).
P.1-1942, Hilliard (Plate 11) and P.40-1935, Holbein (Plate 8)

The Limning Methods of Hornebolte and Holbein

To imagine Hornebolte teaching Holbein limning we can look to Simon Benninck's self-portrait (Plate 9) as a guide, except that Holbein, as a left-handed artist, would have set up the painting slope to face the other way so that his hand did not block the light. In most technical respects Holbein's work is no different from Hornebolte's; he used the circular format, stuck the vellum to a playing-card for extra strength (fig. 6), lay a carnation ground, and used the same blue background and gold edge. Beyond these basic techniques and format however, Holbein's working method and style were very different.

Hornebolte's background was in book illumination. In his portraits he modelled the features with soft gradations of tone, avoiding hard defining edges, gently indicating a likeness rather than the physical presence of the sitter. In contrast, Holbein is the artist who, in his painting of Henry VIII for Whitehall Palace, created the image of Henry by which he is known today, an image of a king intended to 'abash and annihilate' those who looked at it.[22] Miniature painting served a very different function from such grandiose work. Nonetheless, Holbein's approach to miniature, modelling the features from the middle of the face outwards, forming a hard, clear edge, gave these tiny works both the monumentality and dignified presence of his larger works. Hornebolte and Holbein demonstrate how different the effect of working on such a small scale can be.[23]

Levina Teerlinc and 'divers others'

Holbein and Hornebolte died in 1543 and 1544 respectively and their patron Henry VIII died soon after in 1547, the year that Nicholas Hilliard was born. In Hilliard's treatise (c.1598) he claimed Holbein as his inspiration but gave no account of how he learned to limn, and mentions no other limners by name. However, it has been argued that Hilliard could not have understood the basic techniques of miniature painting from external observation of Holbein's miniatures alone.[24] The mystery of Hilliard's tuition aside, there is also the question of who painted the miniatures which date from between the deaths of Holbein and Hornebolte, and Hilliard's work nearly 30 years later. As well as the few miniatures that survive today, evidence of the continuing production of miniature portraits can be seen in the miniature from 1560 of Katherine Grey wearing her husband's miniature (fig. 7); and the report from 1564 of Elizabeth showing the ambassador of Mary Queen of Scots the miniature of her favourite, Robert Dudley.[25]

It has recently been argued that Levina Teerlinc is the link between Henry's reign and Elizabeth's.[26] Teerlinc was the daughter of Simon Benninck (Plate 9), a leading artist of the Ghent-Bruges School. It seems that Benninck never came to England, but his daughter, like the Horneboltes, was recruited into the service of Henry VIII. Court records for 1546 show a fee of £40 a year to 'last...during your Majesty's pleasure' to 'Levyna Terling, paintrix'. Teerlinc was extremely long-lived, serving the crown until her death in 1576, four years after Hilliard first painted Elizabeth I. Records show that Teerlinc's New Year's Day gifts to Queen Elizabeth included single portraits of the queen as well as group images of Elizabeth and her courtiers, although none of these survive.

Despite Teerlinc's longevity few miniatures have emerged, although a group from this date have been identified that seem to share certain characteristics (Plate 10). These have been attributed to her because of their apparent relation to a tiny limning of Elizabeth celebrating Maundy Thursday among her courtiers (private collection). The latter was attributed to Teerlinc because of its similarity to the subject matter of Teerlinc's untraced New Year gifts.

However, unlike the groups of miniatures attributed to Hornebolte and Holbein, there is no consensus that these miniatures are by one hand and that Teerlinc's name can then be attached to them.[27] Hilliard only mentioned Holbein by name, but noted 'yet had the king in wages for limning divers others'. Equally fascinating is Hilliard's reference to a white pigment: 'this white the women painters use'. Teerlinc was not the only daughter of a Ghent-Bruges master in England – Dürer had bought and admired a limning of Christ by Lucas Hornebolte's sister, Susannah. It is possible that Susannah, like her brother, limned portraits at Henry's

Plate 9. Simon Benninck, *Self-Portrait*, 1558. Watercolour on vellum (81 x 53 mm). A sloping easel was used for painting portraits and traditional subjects, such as the Madonna and Child shown here. Both illuminators and miniaturists worked by natural light and without magnification, although Benninck's glasses hint at the strain of such intricate work. P.159-1910

court although unlike Teerlinc her position at court was not as a 'paintrix'. It was Susannah who led a group of ladies to attend Anne of Cleves when she travelled to England to meet her future husband, and also attended Henry's last queen Catherine Parr, whose accounts show payments to the wife of Susannah's brother, Lucas. We cannot lightly dismiss the idea that Susannah was encouraged to paint for her mistress.

Susannah died before 1554 (when her husband remarried), so no miniatures after this date can be attributed to her. Richard Haydocke, writing at the same time as Hilliard offers a further puzzle, by stating that limning

was 'dealt...by some of our Country-men, as Shoote, Bettes, &c.' John Shute described himself as 'architect and painter' and died in 1563 but there is no reason to contradict Haydocke's belief that he also limned. John Bettes is more difficult because there is no definite date for his death, and oil paintings painted in his very idiosyncratic style are unknown after the 1550s. There are references in Catherine Parr's accounts of 1546/7 to Bettes being paid for 'vj pictures being lymmed' and the eighteenth-century antiquarian Vertue recorded a limning by Bettes dated 1548. After this date there is no evidence that he was even alive.[28]

Figure 7. Levina Teerlinc, attributed to, *Katherine Grey*, holding her child and wearing her husband's miniature, *c.*1560. Watercolour on vellum (dia. 51 mm). This is the earliest known depiction of a miniature being worn. Katherine Grey was imprisoned by Elizabeth I for secretly marrying Edward Seymour; both had a claim to the throne, making their child a focus for attempts to usurp Elizabeth.
(Courtesy of the Duke of Rutland)

Plate 10. Levina Teerlinc, attributed to, *Katherine Grey*, c.1555–60. Watercolour on vellum (dia. 33 mm). This miniature exemplifies all the characteristics that have been attributed to Levina Teerlinc: weak draughtsmanship, thin paint, loose brushwork, and the emaciated treatment of the figure, especially in the arms.
P.10-1979

It is worth considering why there are so few miniatures from the reigns of Elizabeth's brother and sister and why no artist with the reputation of Holbein or Hilliard emerged. Teerlinc's salaried position at court may have allowed her to work in a more amateur fashion than Hilliard, who was forced to be more commercially minded. There were also many restraints on creativity at this time: the political and religious climates were unstable during the passing of power from a Protestant child (under the sway of political factions) to a devoutly Catholic queen. Hilliard astutely noted that if a man 'live in time of trouble, and under a savage government wherein arts be not esteemed, and himself but of small means, woe be unto him as unto an untimely birth'. He illustrates his point with the story of an artist neglected during the reigns of Edward and Mary and forced to abandon his art. With 'the liberty of the gospel at the coming in of Queen Elizabeth' he did not return to art but instead became 'a reading minister'.

The art of miniature has been described as an essentially secret art, with a strict line of descent from the Ghent-Bruges School of Hornebolte, who taught Holbein as a favour, through Teerlinc (trained by her father Simon Benninck) who possibly taught Hilliard.[29] Certainly it is not unreasonable to suggest that Teerlinc taught Hilliard. But in the period between Holbein's death and Hilliard's emergence in the 1570s, the documentary evidence and the miniatures themselves show that a healthy scepticism should accompany any attempt to attribute these miniatures to only one artist.

CHAPTER TWO

THE MID-SIXTEENTH TO EARLY SEVENTEENTH CENTURIES

Plate 11 (actual size). Nicholas Hilliard, *Portrait of an Unknown Young Man Aged 24*, 1572. Watercolour on vellum, rectangular (60 x 47 mm). Hilliard retained the traditional way of inscribing miniatures, citing the date as 'Ano Dni 1576' (an abbreviation for 'Anno Domini', 'in the year of our Lord'), and the age of the sitter as 'Aetatis sue XXIIII' (aged 24). The face here has been retouched; the original skin tone would have been paler.
P.1-1942

Hilliard's Boyhood and Formative Experiences

Nicholas Hilliard, born in 1547, the same year that Henry VIII died, was not immune from the turbulent reigns of the Protestant boy king, Edward VI (*r.*1547–53) and his fiercely Catholic sister Mary I (*r.*1553–8). Hilliard's father Richard, a leading goldsmith and citizen of the town of Exeter in Devon (Plate 14), had taken a prominent role in the defence of the city when it was threatened by rioters protesting against Edward VI's Prayer Book. Under Edward, England had been a safe haven for Protestant refugees from the

Continent. Under 'Bloody Mary', however, Protestant refugees fled England, and the young Nicholas Hilliard was one of them.

As was often the custom with sons from families of standing such as the Hilliards, Nicholas, aged about ten, had been placed in the household of the rich merchant family of Richard Bodley who, like Hilliard's father, had taken part in the defence of Exeter. Soon after Nicholas' arrival the household left for the safety of Geneva, now in modern Switzerland, joining a close-knit community of leading Protestant English families. Here he would have learnt French, allowing him later to live and work in France, and is generally assumed to have shared the lessons of Bodley's sons. Indeed Hilliard's fellow student Thomas Bodley was to sit to Hilliard in 1598, the year that he founded the Bodleian Library in Oxford.

It has been argued that Hilliard stayed with the Bodleys in London when they returned to England after the accession of Elizabeth I in 1558, his role in the household possibly that of a page.[1] Three miniatures have traditionally been attributed to the 13-year-old Hilliard (in private collections), two of them supposedly self-portraits. However, one is a later copy of the other, and it is generally agreed that a blue-eyed boy does not turn into a brown-eyed man. The third miniature, however, could be by Hilliard. It is a round portrait of Edward Seymour, Duke of Somerset (who was executed in 1550), set within a painted border inscribed with the date 1560 and the initials 'NH'. This border does not appear to have been added at a later date. The miniature is crude and, with its gold background, is unlike other miniatures of the time. It could, however, be the work of a curious boy who, within the Bodley household, found or was shown an image of the dead Somerset to copy. A book about limning books, published 13 years later in 1573, implies that artists could buy pigments from apothecaries, indicating that while Hilliard would have had to acquire painting equipment, he would not have had to manufacture his own pigments.[3] Considering this level of interest and application, it is significant that no other miniatures have been attributed to Hilliard until he emerged in the 1570s with his own distinctive style.

In 1562, when Nicholas was about 15, his father arranged payment for him to be apprenticed to the Queen's Goldsmith Robert Brandon. For seven years Hilliard would have lived and worked on the bustling row of shops and workshops centred on the Goldsmiths' Company Hall. Attached to a prestigious and busy workshop Hilliard could have been encouraged in any existing interest in miniature painting. The miniature worn by Katherine Grey (fig. 7), set and strung on a necklace, suggests that Hilliard could have seen miniatures brought to the workshop to be mounted. Working for the Queen's Goldsmith, Hilliard was also well-placed to meet those who could have taught him limning.

Hilliard later claimed that Holbein's miniatures had inspired him, but Hilliard's work owes more to his training as a goldsmith. In Brandon's workshop Hilliard would have learned to engrave metal and to copy printed designs. Hilliard tended to use a much paler skin tone

Plate 12. Nicholas Hilliard, *Robert Dudley*, Earl of Leicester. Watercolour on vellum (dia. 44 mm). Robert Dudley, one of Elizabeth's first favourites, was Hilliard's first major patron at court. This is a rare example of a background colour other than the conventional brilliant blue.
E.1174-1988

than his predecessors, over which he hatched in 'imitation of the burin technique of engravers such as Dürer' (see Plate 13).[4] Hilliard's use of burnished metal, his love of decorative flourish and clear precise line all come from his training as a goldsmith.

Hilliard's Early Miniatures and First Patrons

Aged about 22, Hilliard completed his apprenticeship, becoming a Freeman of the Goldsmith Company which entitled him to open his own workshop and employ apprentices. In Hilliard's own words being a goldsmith remained his 'other trade'. It has recently emerged that when living in France for three years he set up a workshop in Paris, where the Parisian Goldsmiths Company is recorded investigating the standard of his work.[5]

Although undated, Hilliard's first miniatures seem to indicate that it was a few years before he established a limning practice. These works, however, are accomplished and confidently experimental in terms of size, shape, background colour, and calligraphy (Plates 11 and 12). At first Hilliard used the traditional round format of earlier miniatures. However, two tiny oval portraits from around 1575 of Queen Elizabeth I and

Opposite: Plate 13.
Nicholas Hilliard, detail of a
portrait of Richard Hilliard
(Plate 14a), c.1571–5.
Watercolour on vellum.
Hilliard invariably used a
much paler skin tone than
his predecessors, and his
use of fine lines contrasts
strikingly with Hornebolte's
soft, indistinct manner.
P.154-1910

Plate 14 a and b. Nicholas
Hilliard. (a) *Richard Hilliard*,
Hilliard's father aged 58.
Watercolour on vellum (dia.
41 mm). (b) *Alice Hilliard*,
Hilliard's wife aged 22,
signed 'NH' twice and dated
1578. Watercolour on vellum
(dia. 59 mm). Along with
Hilliard's self-portrait (front
cover) these two works are
the earliest surviving
examples of such intimate
family portraits by an artist in
England.
(a) P.154-1910; (b) P.2-1942

her favourite, Robert Dudley (private collection), are early examples of the shape that soon became the accepted form of the portrait miniature.[6] The unusual size of these portraits seems to indicate that this secret pair was intended for a particular setting, probably a jewel.

The rectangular shape seen in Plate 11 was equally experimental. This unknown young man dated 1572, formerly paired with his wife (private collection), could have been intended for a 'booke', an Elizabethan jewel, literally like a small book, worn on a chain from a girdle at the waist. But if the queen, who first sat to Hilliard in 1572, allowed Hilliard to see her collection of miniatures, he may have been influenced by the work of miniaturists outside England. We know from an account of the Scottish ambassador in 1564 that Elizabeth had a miniature of Mary Queen of Scots who, until she was widowed in 1561, lived with her husband the Dauphin at the French court.[7] A miniature by Clouet of Mary in the Royal Collection that survives today is rectangular.

Hilliard's first sitting with the queen, probably won through his patron, Robert Dudley, must have raised great hopes for the future. In his treatise Hilliard recalled the day 'when first I came in her Highness's presence to draw', as well as his discussions with Elizabeth about art, especially 'shadowing' which led to Elizabeth's decision to be painted in 'the open alley of a goodly garden, where no tree was near'. The queen was an interested sitter and Hilliard faced 'divers other like questions in art by her most excellent Majesty'. But while Hilliard wanted the status and security of a salaried position like Holbein, Hornebolte and Teerlinc before him, the crown had squandered money during and after Henry VIII's reign. Hilliard was employed only when he was needed, forcing him to set up a workshop in the city. Hilliard's 'unknown' sitters are as likely to be obscure gentlemen and ladies visiting London, or citizens of London, as the elite of the court.

Hilliard in France

Hilliard wrote with bitterness of a life without the 'pension or reward of princes', forced to promote his work by ruses such as painting 'a rare piece of work' to give 'to some worthy personage', just to 'be spoken of'. In 1576 Hilliard travelled to France in the train of the English ambassador, probably on the queen's business and, despite the queen's letters to her ambassador enquiring when Hilliard intended to return, he stayed for three years. The ambassador assured Elizabeth that Hilliard intended only 'to increase his knowledge by this voyage' and 'to get a piece of money of the lords and ladies here for his better maintenance in England at his return'.[8] Indeed Hilliard worked in many of the leading aristocratic households, met with fellow artists, and in his own words travelled to 'confer with wise men'. His self-portrait (front cover) is a virtuoso performance, asserting that he is no mere artisan but an artist worthy to keep company with princes. Although Hilliard met with encouragement in France he was not financially successful. Before he had left for France he had married Alice Brandon (plate 14), daughter of his old master, who travelled with him, and in 1578 he finally returned to England on the birth of the first of their seven children. In thinly disguised autobiography Hilliard wrote that artists, 'having commonly many children if they be married', were invariably forced to 'profit by other trade'. He set up shop in Gutter Lane at the sign of the Maidenhead and returned to his old life, supplementing limning 'by other trade'.

Hilliard's Workshop

Hilliard's treatise offers some fascinating insights into his working life. In choosing a workshop in London he would have selected an area away from his fellow goldsmiths, a 'place where neither dust, smoke, noise nor stench may offend', since some colours could not 'endure some airs, especially in the sulphurous air of seacoal and the gilding of goldsmiths'. Hilliard was perhaps the earliest artist to associate the discoloration of pigments with sulphurous pollution.[9]

For Hilliard, 'the place where you work' (he does not use the modern word 'studio') should be lit from the north-east by one window only but it should be 'great and fair' with no walls or trees blocking the light. It would have been difficult for Hilliard to find a room to meet these exacting demands among the late medieval domestic buildings of London, constructed so that each floor extended beyond the one below thereby blocking daylight. Hilliard would have had to choose an upper floor, preferably overlooking an open space or garden.

Hilliard claimed that limning required a life of temperance, with no 'violent exercise in sports' although a little dancing or bowling was allowed. Many of Hilliard's comments about artists reflected his belief that limning was a genteel practice. He wanted to create an atmosphere for his sitters that would also reflect well on him: 'A good painter hath tender senses' and required 'sweet odours' to 'comfort the brain'. This in part explains his concern to be separate from the noisy, smelly workshops of other crafts.

Hilliard and his Sitters

A first sitting could take between two and four hours, a second as long as eight, and the last a further three hours. Hilliard was acutely aware of the potential boredom of both sitter and artist and noted that 'discreet talk or reading, quiet mirth or music…shorten the time and quicken the spirit, both in the drawer and he which is drawn'. Presumably servants and friends of the sitter could attend to read or make music.

He would have worked at a table with an easel very like that in Plate 9, with the sitter seated about two yards away. For full-lengths he would first draw the head in this position, then place the sitter standing six yards away to draw the rest of the figure. Clearly sitters such as the queen would not have visited Hilliard in his studio. For Hilliard's first sitting with Elizabeth I in her garden, he would have used a portable painting box.

Hilliard recalls with some pride conversations about his art with eminent sitters such as Sir Philip Sidney, 'that noble and most valiant knight, that great scholar and excellent poet'. However, clearly aggravated by the questions and opinions of some of his sitters, he commented that to 'avoid anger' an artist must 'shut out questioners or busy fingers'. Limning, Hilliard believed, was for 'noble persons very meet', and he was content with the 'better and wiser sort' who made occasional well-judged comments. But on occasions he had to endure 'ridiculous, absurd speeches' from the 'ignoranter and baser sort', who were commonly 'servants' and criticised partly to 'flatter' the sitter and partly to show

Plate 15 a and b. Nicholas Hilliard, (a) *Unknown Woman*, *c.*1590-93. Watercolour on vellum (59 x 47 mm). (b) Unknown Woman, said to be 'Mistress Holland', 1593. Watercolour on vellum (58 x 48 mm). Here we can see Hilliard's close attention to costume and the impact of ever-changing fashions on his miniatures. Mrs Holland's costume is delightfully simple, her only decoration the embroidered bees and deer on her stomacher; the dress of the unknown lady is more elaborate with details such as the red textile ties on her ruff.
(a) P.9-1947; (b) P.134-1910;

'how bold they may be to speak their opinion'. Hilliard advised the artist to work on in silence.

These observations concern mostly Hilliard's choices as an artist, such as the difficulty of catching 'those lovely graces, witty smilings, and those stolen glances which suddenly like lightning pass and another countenance taketh place', or how 'when you spy a good grace in their hand take it quickly' without telling the sitter for fear that they adopt an 'unnatural or affected grace'. But a sitter could have an impact on the appearance of a miniature just in their choice of clothes (Plate 15). Hilliard and Oliver both seem to have faithfully recorded costumes; indeed the elaborate outfit worn by Richard Sackville is a rare instance where the clothes worn can actually be identified in a contemporary inventory (Plate 16).[10] It is likely that, to avoid tiring the sitter, such costumes were taken to the workshop at a later date for the limner to work on separately.

The Miniature within Elizabethan Court Culture

Some commissions demanded more than simple likenesses. Hilliard's images of Elizabeth I from the 1580s onwards are not straightforward portraits of a 50-year-old woman vainly decked out in her court finery (Plates 22, 29, 30 and 31). England faced an uncertain future both immediate and long-term: at war with Spain and threatened with invasion, with an ageing and heirless queen. Hilliard either intuitively understood the mood of the day or discussed the matter with the queen's ministers, for he deliberately avoided painting the reality of an ageing woman. Instead his image is of an ageless 'Virgin Queen', her features rejuvenated by reducing them to a few schematic lines. Framed by the opulence of her costume, she is no longer a mortal threatened by death but an icon of enduring youth and power.

Other portraits, with their elaborate symbolism and mottos (Plate 17), equally reveal a close co-operation between artist and sitter. This move towards symbolism also developed in part from the unique quality of a court ruled by a woman. Elizabeth exerted her authority under the guise of elaborate rituals of courtship with her male courtiers. This role-playing was brought to a pitch at the Accession Day ceremonial jousts, at which the queen's dominant role was displayed, not as her father could have done by testing his strength on the field, but by receiving the homage of her knights. Each courtier presented her with a shield bearing an 'impressa', a

combination of picture and motto 'borne by Noble personages...to notifie some particular conceit of their own', namely their service to the queen.[11]

Young Man Among Roses (Plate 18) shows how Hilliard and his sitters contrived to incorporate this chivalrous concept into the miniature portrait. Hand on heart, the youth declares his devotion to the queen, wearing her colours of black and white and embraced by the delicate white eglantine rose, also symbolic of the queen. The latin motto 'Dat poenas laudata fides' is a tiny extract from a speech out of Lucan's *De Bello Civili*, which the sitter could have expected the recipient of this miniature to recognise and understand as a message of faithful love and loyalty. It has been argued that the young man is Robert Devereux, 2nd Earl of Essex, who, at 17, was the 60-year-old queen's new favourite.

In miniatures of a more conventional size, the symbolic nature of the impressa and portrait united to create a particularly intimate, even secret, image shared by the sitter and the intended owner. In fact, while most sitters probably had very particular ideas, there were also books illustrating and explaining emblems which Hilliard could have used to offer suggestions. Clasped hands (Plate 17) were, for example, a relatively well-known symbol of concord and plighted faith. The motto, however, does baffle the casual viewer: 'Attici amoris ergo' has long been resistant to translation let alone explanation.

Hillard's Studio and Isaac Oliver, his 'well profitting scholar'

In the 1590s Isaac Oliver (fig. 8) became a formidable rival to his former teacher Hilliard. Unlike Hilliard, whose forceful personality emerges through legal disputes with colleagues, letters to his patrons, and through his treatise, there is little documentary evidence of the apparently more quiet Oliver. According to Richard Haydocke, Oliver was Hilliard's 'well profitting scholar', and not an apprentice bound to his master for

Plate 16 (actual size). Isaac Oliver, *Richard Sackville*, 3rd Earl of Dorset. 1616. Watercolour on vellum, rectangular (235 x 153 mm). The outfit worn by Sackville in this miniature has been identified in 'An Inventorie of the rich wearing apparrell of the right hnorable richard Earle of Dorset': 'puffs of blew velvett...with sonnes Moones and starres of gold'. Costumes were possibly taken to the studio to be worked on separately, to avoid boring the sitter.
721-1882

Plate 17a and b. Nicholas Hilliard: (a) *Young Man Against a Flame Background*. Watercolour on vellum (69 x 54 mm). Above: (b) *Young Man Clasping a Hand From a Cloud,* 1588. Watercolour on vellum (60 x 50 mm). Both these miniatures suggest the involvement of the sitter in the chosen symbolism.

This must have been particularly true of the intimate portrait of the man against shimmering flames, in a state of undress and wearing a mysterious jewel. (This miniature has sometimes been attributed to Isaac Oliver.)
(a) P.5-1917; (b) P.21-1942

Opposite: Plate 18. Nicholas Hilliard, *Young Man Among Roses*, c.1587. Watercolour on vellum (136 x 73 mm). This famous image is the most elaborate example of how the chivalry of Elizabeth's court influenced the portrait miniature. Wearing Elizabeth's colours (black and white) and embraced by the eglantine rose, also symbolic of Elizabeth, this youth, with hand on heart, declares his devotion to his queen.
P.163-1910

Plate 19. Nicholas Hilliard, *Unknown Woman from the City*, 1602. Watercolour on vellum (60 x 46 mm). The Latin inscription 'Videtur et Vere est' ('it seems and truely is') shows how the taste for enigmatic mottos was not confined to the court. The ivory box, without its lid, is probably contemporary. Such boxes could have been worn in a small pouch hanging from a woman's waist.

Plate 20. Nicholas Hilliard, *Unknown Young Man*, c.1588. Watercolour on vellum (55 x 44 mm). With his gold earring and rakish beard, this young man seems the epitome of an Elizabethan gentleman. Datable to the same year as the *Young Man Clasping a Hand From a Cloud* (Plate 17), this portrait demonstrates a simple alternative to the complex symbolism of many court portraits.
P.15-1977

seven long years. Oliver was born about 1560, the son of Pierre Olivier, a goldsmith from Rouen, part of a community of French protestants forced to move around Europe to escape bouts of persecution in France. The Oliviers were recorded in London when Isaac was about eight and again when he was 17. An indistinct date and inscription on a drawing of the 'Lamentation of the Dead Christ' implies that in 1586, aged about 26, Oliver was in Tournai, France.[12] Thus while we do not know where Oliver was living between the ages of 17 and 27 when he came to Hilliard's workshop, he had clearly had some training as an artist; his presumably financial arrangement with Hilliard was simply to learn limning, an art clearly favoured in England.

Hilliard's rather random but expressive practical instruction in his treatise gives a flavour of how he would probably have taught his new 'scholar'. First Oliver would have been instructed in the preparation of the parchment (animal skin), the 'best thing to limn on', especially 'virgin parchment…such as never bore hair…some call it vellum, some abertive, derived from the word abortive for untimely birth'. Oliver would then have learned how to paste it with starch glue to 'paste-board', usually a playing-card, to form a rectangular tablet (fig. 6), burnishing it until it was 'very smooth and white'.

Next Hilliard would have taught Oliver how to lay the 'carnation' ground, the flesh colour of the face. 'Choose your carnations too fair' explains Hilliard, for if the complexion is 'too brown you shall never work it fair enough'. Limning required care, working 'little and little at the first' since 'botching or mending will be perceived'. But limning also require speed, confidence and fine judgement. Using a broad brush made of squir-

Figure 8. Hendrik Hondius II, *Isaac Oliver*. Engraving (20.2 x 12 cm). Isaac Oliver was French by birth and sought his artistic inspiration from the Continent; it is thus appropriate that his portrait appears as part of a series of mostly Continental artists.
E.5403-1919

Figure 9. This display of limners' materials was reconstructed by V. J. Murrell for the exhibition 'Artists of the Tudor Court', V&A, 1983. It includes mussel shells smeared with pigments ground with gum arabic ready for painting; paint brushes (at this time called 'pencils') made from dark squirrel hair set in bird quills and mounted on wooden sticks; a mother of pearl palette; two burnishers, the larger being a canine tooth used to burnish the vellum and card tablets, the smaller a stoat tooth for burnishing small areas of gold.

Plate 21a and b. (a) Isaac Oliver, *Sir Arundel Talbot*, 1596. Watercolour on vellum (69 x 54 mm).
(b) Nicholas Hilliard, *Unknown Woman*, c.1575–80. Watercolour on vellum (39 x 33 mm). Both these works show what might have been achieved after two of the three sittings working directly onto the vellum. The features have begun to be modelled over the carnation using hatches of red and brown, but more detail is needed. The Oliver has not been trimmed and the dress is incomplete; in the Hilliard the hair has been loosely washed over the carnation to suggest how it should look.
(a)P.4-1917; (b)P.8-1947

rel hair the carnation was 'laid flowing', not too flowing that the card became wrinkled ('cockled'), but enough that it could be completed before any part dried 'patched and rough'. Interestingly, a later writer on limning, Edward Norgate, recommended that vellum tablets could be prepared with different types of carnation to fit the complexions of possible sitters. This relieved the artist from having to achieve a perfect carnation during a sitting and spared the sitter the boredom of this time-consuming process (Plate 21).

Oliver would have learned to prepare his own colours, finely grinding each pigment on a little grinding stone, 'washing' some to separate out larger impurities and drying these briefly in the sun. The pigments were then stored 'in a paper or a box' and only mixed with gum arabic and water in little mussel shells when needed. The process of preparing his own pigments allowed the artist to create precisely certain effects, such as different thicknesses of white, the thickest used to create the three-dimensional effect of a crisp white ruff (Plate 22).

Unlike Norgate, Hilliard offered no shortcuts in preparation for a sitting and condemned limners who, in trying to spare 'time and cost', 'work out of their old shells of colours, though they be...dusty'. Hilliard was very particular: 'the first and chiefest precept which I give is cleanliness', and he would have advised Oliver to wear

Opposite: Plate 22. Nicholas Hilliard, *Elizabeth I*. Watercolour on vellum. To achieve the appearance of starched lace Hilliard dribbled thick paint on to the surface, creating a relief pattern that actually casts a shadow. The ruby would have been created by laying a ground of burnished silver, over which Hilliard modelled the jewel out of stained resin. Some silver details such as the highlights on the pearls appear black from tarnishing.
622-1882

Plate 23 a and b. (a) Isaac Oliver, *Man in Black*, c.1590–1600, watercolour on vellum (51 x 41 mm). (b) Nicholas Hilliard, *Young Man with Bonnet and Feather*, c.1585-90. Watercolour on vellum (51 x41 mm). These portraits show the very different ways in which Hilliard and Oliver painted their sitters' features. Oliver used shadowing to create the deep-set eyes, a protruding nose and prominent cheekbones. Hilliard's approach was much more schematic – a few lines hinting at distinguishing facial features.
(a) P.50-1941; (b) P.4-1974

silk 'such as sheddeth least dust or hairs' and to 'take heed of the dandruff of the head'. He also would have warned Oliver of the dangers of touching the miniature's surface, of breathing on it 'especially in cold weather', and 'of speaking over your work for sparkling…of spittle', all of which could spoil this delicate water-based art.

Limning was an intricate art, hard on the eyes as the glasses worn by Benninck in his self-portrait testify (Plate 9). But no limner seems to have used magnification which would have distorted the work when viewed with the naked eye. Hilliard's only advice on this matter was that the ability to limn was a gift from God, the limner should take care of himself 'lest [this gift] be soon taken' and one's 'sight or steadiness of hand decay'.

In his treatise Hilliard rightly claimed that his innovative techniques for painting jewels were 'no part of limning'. However, pride perhaps spurred him to share how he painted pearls: a raised blob of white lead with some shadowing to one side, crowned with a rounded touch of silver paint, was then burnished 'with a pretty little tooth of some ferret or stoat or other wild little beast' (Plate 22). Oliver was clearly privy to the secrets of Hilliard's transparent stones, such as rubies, created by laying a ground of silver burnished to a shine, over which a heated needle was used to model the jewel out of stained resin. And yet, Oliver's first-known miniature, dating from 1587, is quite unlike Hilliard's bright jewel-like work, showing instead the influence of the very different small oval portrait prints by the Netherlandish artist Hendrik Goltzius. The sophisticated portrait of an unknown man aged 27 (Plate 24) also shows this influence.

Oliver as an Independent Artist

From the start Oliver conspicuously looked beyond Hilliard to the Continent. After Hilliard's three-year sojourn in France from 1576 to 1578 he became as insular as most of English society during the 1580s. To Hilliard his three-dimensional way of painting was a superior art which 'seemeth to be the thing itself, even the work of God and not of man'. On the Continent artists worked very differently, using optical tricks to render flat two-dimensional works (on paper or panel) three-dimensional. They used scientific perspective to give the appearance of looking into a space rather than at a flat surface; and *chiaroscuro*, the Italian for the contrast between light and shade (shadowing), to create

depth and dimension so that the skull beneath the flesh is apparent (Plate 23).

Hilliard was clearly aware of the art and practices of the Continent. He praised Goltzius, and rather confusedly discussed perspective and shadowing. But he was unwilling to follow scientific rules, claiming that perspective simply was 'an art taken for or by the effect or judgement of the eye'. Hilliard's patrons were probably unaware of his misconceived perspective, seen particularly in his full-length portraits. Sir John Harrington indicates how strange such practices were to English eyes, describing perspective as a 'curious effect of seemingly looking into the distance and which not everyone will observe'.[13] Since Hilliard's miniatures were invariably elegant, except perhaps his tiny full-length *Sir Christopher Hatton* (Plate 25), his mistakes are rarely glaringly obvious.

Oliver was undoubtedly more comfortable with the complicated and expensive full-length format. Throughout his life, Oliver worked privately on drawings as well as subject limnings, such as a Madonna and Child that took him over three years to complete.[14] Such works were not unusual in Continental terms, but within an English context they were revolutionary. There was no market for such works, although two simple but unique small miniatures, the *Head of Christ* (Plate 3) and *The Goddess Diana* (Plate 26), may have been commissioned by an English patron. But Oliver's interest in and knowledge of Continental art practices gave him a compositional inventiveness, and above all confidence, that enhanced his larger portrait miniatures, such as the so-called *Frances Howard* (Plate 27). He was able to place a number of figures together, or place a figure lying on a bank in a landscape, using aerial perspective to convince the eye that a flat surface in fact recedes.

How pragmatic Oliver had to be to survive the artistic climate of England can be seen by comparing his portrait of a young man (Plate 24), painted in 1590, with the portraits of two little girls painted the same year (Plate 28). The man is confidently in Oliver's own style, whereas the girls are very much in the mode of Hilliard's work, and were undoubtedly a response to the specific desires of the patron.

The Settings and Uses of the Miniature

Today large limnings such as *Richard Sackville* (Plate 16) and *Frances Howard* (Plate 27) are known as 'cabinet'

Plate 24 (actual size). Isaac Oliver, *Unknown Man Aged 27*, 1590. Watercolour on vellum (54 x 44 mm). Oliver could paint miniatures in the same jewel-like style as Hilliard (Plate 28), but he was probably also trained in Continental art and could produce very different work, such as this miniature showing the influence of the Netherlandish print-maker Hendrik Goltzius.
P.37-1941

Plate 25 (actual size). Nicholas Hilliard, *Sir Christopher Hatton*, c.1588–91. Watercolour on vellum (56 x 43 mm). Hilliard experimented with full-length miniatures, and this is one of the few painted on this scale. Elizabeth's Lord Chancellor is shown in the full regalia of his office, yet the effect is perhaps not as dignified as the sitter would have hoped.
P.138-1910

miniatures, a recent term describing the way in which such limnings were kept in either a cupboard or room hung with similar small paintings. The more intimate small oval, however, continued as the favourite shape and size. Today only a few very elaborate jewelled lockets survive from this period (Plates 29, 30 and 31), but simple lockets were probably the most common setting for a miniature – the whole often referred to as a 'Jewel'. In Shakespeare's *Twelfth Night* (c.1600), Olivia, in love with Viola who is disguised as a man, gives her a miniature, saying, 'Here wear this jewel for me 'tis my picture – Refuse it not, it hath no tongue to vex you'. Shakespeare exploits the frisson of the miniature as an intimate gift, to be kept secret or revealed. A possibly apocryphal story tells how Queen Elizabeth demanded to see whose portrait was hidden in a locket worn by one of her ladies, and then pinned the locket on to her own shoe buckle. Thus she began an elaborate play with the young male courtier whose picture it was. He, understanding the favour the queen had shown him, wrote a poem of thanks whereupon she pinned the miniature at her elbow close to her heart.[15]

Many Elizabethan oil portraits seem to play on this secrecy, with the sitter wearing what could be a locket, but closed or turned towards their body. In a portrait of Francis Drake he wears a carved onyx jewel, known today as the 'Drake Jewel' (private collection, on loan to the V&A).[16] The back opens to reveal what cannot be seen in his portrait – a miniature of Elizabeth I. If the jewel worn by the young man in Plate 17 survived today, it too might reveal a secret miniature. Today, when contemplating these tiny portraits, we have to remember the person for whom they would have been intended. John Donne memorably captured the intimacy of the tiny miniature in his poem *Elegie: His Picture*. Himself a young adventurer sailing in 1596 with Hilliard's patron the Earl of Essex, Donne pays tribute to the miniature as a last gift between lovers before parting: 'Here take my Picture; though I bid farewell, Thine, in my heart, where my soule dwells, shall dwell…When weather-beaten I come back, my hand perhaps with rude oares torne, or sun-beams tann'd', with white hair and skin stained with gunpowder, 'if rival fooles taxe thee to have lov'd a man so foule, and coarse…This shall say what I was'.

Plate 26. Isaac Oliver, *The Goddess Diana*, 1615. Watercolour on sized cambric laid down on to a thin panel of limewood (86 x 64 mm). This unusual miniature, painted on cambric rather than vellum, would probably be unattributable were it not signed 'IO'. P.9-1940

Opposite: Plate 27. Isaac Oliver, *Unknown Woman*, known as *Frances Howard*, c.1596–1600. Watercolour on vellum (dia. 130 mm). This is one of Oliver's masterpieces: a virtuoso performance of *chiaroscuro* (light and shade): the colours graduating within a very subtle range from grey into grey-black, touched with white, gold and silver. Sadly the red pigment has faded and one can only imagine the warmth of her cheeks and lips in this otherwise cool image. P.12-1971

Plate 28. Isaac Oliver, *Two Unknown Girls*, one aged four and one aged five, 1590. Watercolour on vellum (54 x 43 mm). Portraits of children were extremely rare at this time so these two girls probably belonged to an important family. The portraits were conceived as a pair: one holding a carnation and smiling, the other holding an apple and frowning. It is likely that the patron decided on this singular symbolism with the artist.
P.145,146-1910

Plates 29 and 30. The Heneage ('Armada') Jewel containing a portrait miniature, *Elizabeth I,* by Nicholas Hilliard *c.*1600. Gold and enamel with diamonds and rubies (height 70 mm). The medallic image of the queen, the ark, the miniature and the two lids unite into one jewel. Such an intricate setting is typical of the layered symbolism of the Elizabethan period. This elaborate setting is one of a few that survived being broken up for their precious elements.
M.81-1935

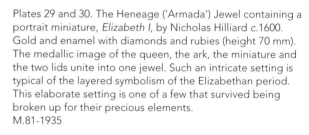

Plate 31. Nicholas Hilliard, *Elizabeth I*, *c*.1600. Watercolour on vellum (62 x 47mm). This miniature was originally acquired by the V&A for its elaborate locket, which has an open-work front of gold set with jewels and a scrolled enamelled back. This miniature is also unusual in showing the queen with her hair flowing freely, indicating her virginity.
4404-1857

CHAPTER THREE

THE EARLY SEVENTEENTH CENTURY

The New Stuart Dynasty

When in 1603 James VI of Scotland became James I of England, he offered the nation the security of unquestioned dynastic roots via his mother, Mary Queen of Scots (who like Elizabeth I was a grand-daughter of Henry VII); and a hopeful dynastic future in the form of his young heir, Prince Henry, and a marriageable daughter, Elizabeth. James, even more enthusiastically than his predecessor, embraced the portrait as a way of promoting the new Stuart dynasty. When the historian Thomas Lyte gave James a manuscript tracing the king's dynastic roots he was rewarded with a miniature of King James by Hilliard in a magnificent locket known today as the *Lyte Jewel* (British Museum).

The miniature was particularly suited to the monarchy, offering a precious image of the king, small enough to be awarded personally in a public ceremony, and worn to mark the king's favour and the courtier's loyalty. Philip Gawdy wrote to his brother about one such ceremony: 'some knights and other gentlemen of the King's servants to number of sixteen had chains given them by the King with his picture hanging by to the value of some thirty or forty pound. All the rest had his picture only'. James' patronage of the miniature encouraged another type of small portrait, the silver medallion (fig. 10). It has therefore been suggested that the works on chains could have been medallions, while the 'picture only' may have been a miniature which the recipient would have had set.[1]

Hilliard and James I

Nicholas Hilliard was retained as the King's limner, but employed primarily in the tedious process of providing repetitions of the king's portrait. As will be discussed later, the sheer number of 'Hilliardesque' portraits of James I and his family imply that the 56-year-old Hilliard almost certainly had assistance (Plate 32). However it has been suggested that Hilliard did not enjoy painting portraits of James, and that poor works could still be the

Figure 10 (actual size). Simon Van de Passe, early 17th century (60 x 50 mm). Silver medallion depicting James I, Anne of Denmark, Prince Henry. Van de Passe was an engraver who specialised in small black-and-white oval portraits. Using gold or silver he created precious versions of the metal plates from which prints were taken. These were then worn much like miniatures. 126-1865

Opposite: Plate 32. This frame contains six miniature portraits of the family of James I, by Nicholas Hilliard and Isaac Oliver or their studios, assembled c.1625–50 (275 x 194 mm). From the top left: *James I*; *Anne of Denmark*, his queen; *Prince Henry*, his son and heir who died in 1612; *Prince Charles*, his other son who became Charles I; *The King of Bohemia*, his son-in-law; and *Elizabeth, Queen of Bohemia*, his daughter. P.147-152-1910

work of Hilliard himself.[2] Reports abound about the king's rather unpleasant physical characteristics, and it seems that James too, for all his enthusiasm for promoting the monarchy, disliked sitting for his picture. Sir Anthony Weldon stated, 'This Kings character is much easier to take than his picture, for he could never be brought to sit for the taking of that, which is the reason of so few good pieces of him.'[3] The occasional sitting seems to have sufficed to allow Hilliard's studio to update the king's portrait from 1603 until Hilliard's death in 1619.

Isaac Oliver and the Queen, Anne of Denmark

The queen, Anne of Denmark, had her own household and court and was passionately interested in the arts; she encouraged a court style quite different from that of her husband or Elizabeth I. The courtly heroics of Elizabeth's Accession Tilts gave way to the Court Masque, celebrating the Stuart Dynasty through verse, song, music, and scenic spectacle designed by Inigo Jones. Jones, like Isaac Oliver, had been in Italy in the 1590s and gently introduced the English court to the visual language of Renaissance Italy. Oliver, appointed the 'Queens painter for the Art of limning' in 1605, would have found this a more sympathetic atmosphere, and yet it did not significantly alter his patronage. His portrait of a court masquer (Plate 33) is a straightforward depiction of Inigo Jones' costume design, while *Richard Sackville* (Plate 16), with the references to the tiltyard in the discarded armour, is an essentially Elizabethan image despite dating from 1616.

Isaac Oliver and Henry, Prince of Wales

Isaac Oliver was also briefly limner for Henry, Prince of Wales. The prince was nine when his father inherited the throne. In 1610, aged 16, this dynamic young man was invested as Prince of Wales, with his own revenues, household and palaces. Henry was also keenly interested in art and his court became a focus for like-minded collectors. Payments to Oliver in the prince's accounts have suggested that Oliver may have had a new role in the prince's household as an art buyer and even as an oil painter.[4] The evidence, however, is open to interpretation, and whatever hopes Oliver may have had of his young patron they were dashed by the prince's unexpected death on 6 November 1612, aged only 18. Prince

Charles, now heir to the throne, was only 12. Only after Oliver's death did Charles' love of painting develop, and he was later to buy one of Oliver's unusual subject limnings from the painter's son.[5]

Oliver's personal artistic interests were at odds with the desires of most of his English patrons generally; at heart a Continental, rather than English, artist, on one occasion he significantly inscribed the back of a miniature 'Isacq Oliuiero Francese', identifying himself as French.[6]

Limning as an Amateur Art

Two somewhat naive miniatures in the V&A, one signed 'BG' and the other signed 'P', represent the beginning of amateur interest in limning. The Prince Charles signed BG (Plate 34b) is by Balthazar Gerbier, probably painted from a print rather than life. Gerbier only came to England from the Netherlands in 1616, soon afterwards becoming an art buyer and adviser to the Duke of Buckingham.[7] The miniature of James I signed 'P' has recently been attributed to Sir William Palmer, Gentleman to the Bed Chamber of James I (Plate 34a).[8]

Palmer was a herald, an official responsible for keeping a register of marriages, births and deaths for noble families, and devising coats of arms which he then limned. Heraldry was a highly valued art since it was a record of a family's history and position in society. Heraldry and portrait miniatures both used the same materials and in their different ways were a record of a family. This sense of complementary roles can be seen both in a group of separately painted portraits gathered together to represent the Stuart dynasty (Plate 32), and in a large manuscript literally depicting the family 'tree' of Thomas Sackville, 1st Earl of Dorset, with the patron and his wife represented by two miniatures tied to the topmost branches (V&A).

Despite Palmer's heraldic limning his, and Gerbier's, limning as a private practice was unusual. Even connoisseurial interest in art was rare at this time, while the practice of painting was considered the province of the artisan, certainly not the gentleman. Hilliard had tried to raise his status as an artist by arguing in his treatise that 'none should meddle with limning but gentlemen alone'.

Opposite: Plate 33. Isaac Oliver, *Lady Masquer*, 1609. Watercolour on vellum (64 x 51 mm). The Stuart court encouraged a new kind of festival, the masque: a mixture of verse, song, mime, dance and scenic spectacle. P.3-1942

In 1612 Henry Peacham published *Graphice or the Most ancient and Excelent Art of Drawing and Limning*, tellingly reprinted the same year under the title *The Gentlemans Exercise*. Peacham was a tutor to the sons of nobility and an amateur artist. His book was one of a number concerned with the educational ideals and conduct of gentlemen, seeking to temper the old ideal of the warrior knight with that of an intellectually and culturally refined 'gentleman'. Prince Henry, depicted in numerous portraits as a young knight but who was also a collector of Italian and Netherlandish art, exemplifies the meeting of these two ideals at this date. Writing in 1605 Sir Francis Bacon suggested three reasons why 'men have entered into a desire for learning and knowledge': firstly a 'natural curiosity and inquisitive appetite', secondly 'sometimes to entertain their minds with variety and delight', and lastly 'sometimes for ornament and reputation'. Bacon, however, believed there was only one legitimate reason, 'benefit and use'.[9] Peacham, understanding what was essentially a continuing Protestant suspicion of art, argued that gentlemen should learn to draw because it was useful for travel and for war, and he added two chapters: 'on the blazon of arms' (heraldry) and 'on Impresse', the chivalric symbolism employed on shields, allying limning to an art of the governing elite. However, hopeful that interest might grow from such

Plate 34 a and b. (a) Sir James Palmer, *James I*, 1623. Watercolour on vellum (49 x 40 mm). (b) Balthazar Gerbier, *Charles, Prince of Wales*, c.1618–20. Watercolour on vellum (50 x 39 mm). These miniatures are by amateurs, which explains their somewhat rough and awkward quality. Amateur interest in limning was encouraged by books such as Peacham's

Graphice, which advised, 'If you would get further experience, acquaint your-self with some of our excellent masters about London'. (a) P.47-1935; (b) P.12-1958

beginnings, he added, 'if you would get farther experience, acquaint your selfe with some of our excellent Masters about London, where there are many passing judicious and skilfull'.[10]

Writing of his own practice of limning, Peacham noted that he had 'bestowed many idle hours in this well-busied art which perhaps might have beene worse spent'.[11] An air of apology is also found in Edward Norgate's treatise *Miniatura, or the Art of Limning*: 'never was it my meaning that the time spent in this art should become a hindrance to better studies...for all painting in general I look upon but as lace and ornament'. However, when Charles I became king, interest in art began to spread. Palmer and even Norgate became, like Gerbier, advisers on art for leading noblemen and the king. Palmer is known to have limned tiny versions of Charles' paintings.[12] Increasingly, limning as an amateur art loosened its links with heraldry and became part of a wider appreciation of art. By the second half of the seventeenth century, limning was established as a genteel art.

Hilliard's Apprentices

The insatiable demands of the new Royal Family for portraiture raises the question of who was responsible for the many versions of miniatures originally by Hilliard or Oliver. Peacham confirmed the pre-eminence of these two limners, 'old Mr Hilliard, Mr Isaac Oliver inferior to none in Christendom for the countenance in small'. But in 1601 Hilliard wrote to his patron at court, Robert Cecil, to complain that 'hoping to bring up others also for Her majesty's better service, I have taught divers both strangers [foreigners] and English, which now and of a long time have pleased the common sort exceeding well, so that I am myself unable by my art, any longer to keep house in London, without some further help of her Majesty'.[13] Such petitions invariably exaggerated, but nonetheless, over 30 years Hilliard had probably trained a significant number of 'others'. The names of Hilliard's official apprentices, and details of money paid to Hilliard for taking them on, were recorded by the Goldsmiths' Company. These boys probably intended to be goldsmiths as much as limners. Eventually, however, others came to Hilliard to learn limning. According to early eighteenth-century writers, John Bettes the younger, the son of the painter, trained with Hilliard. If so, this is an example of an informal arrangement since Bettes became a freeman of the Painter-Stainers'

company rather than the Goldsmiths'. Similarly, Isaac Oliver, as a foreigner, is not recorded by any guild. Hilliard himself claimed to have trained 'strangers' (foreigners) and a recently discovered will of Pieter Mattheus (1588) shows that he left his 'books of arts' and that which 'concerneth' his art, presumably his painting equipment, to his 'two fellows Isaac Olivyer and Rouland Lacq [Rowland Lockey]'. This suggests that other such arrangements could yet be unearthed.[14]

Rowland Lockey joined Hilliard in 1581, his apprenticeship paid by his father, a crossbow maker and near neighbour of the Hilliards. There are no signed miniatures by Lockey, but he clearly had some training in oil since a large copy of Holbein's *Thomas More and Family* is signed by him (private collection). On the basis of this connection a large limning of the same picture dating from the 1590s (V&A) has been attributed to Lockey. However, without any signed limnings it is too easy to attribute works in the Hilliard style to Lockey. Lockey himself taught his brother Nicholas to limn, and others trained by Hilliard could in turn have passed their knowledge on to others.[15]

Hilliard's concern about the 'divers others' he had trained was less for himself than for his son, Laurence, whose future he tried to secure in his letters to Robert Cecil. Laurence was apparently an unwilling student and Hilliard complained that he could not keep his son 'to it' and asked Cecil to give him a place as a secretary. Cecil's advice was to persevere and ultimately Laurence did become the King's limner on his father's death in 1619, the patent stating that 'we have had sufficient experience of his work for ourself and for our dearest wife the Queen'. However, in a petition to the king in 1621, Laurence claimed that having been attacked by four 'turbulent and mutinous' men in Fleet Street, he was too disabled 'to doe your majesties service and to get his maintenance and living in the arte and profession of lymninge'.[16] The ruse failed when one 'attacker' accused him of lying and the matter was quietly forgotten. Nonetheless, miniatures by Laurence are rare, indicating his continuing lack of commitment to limning.

John Hoskins and the London Art Scene

In 1625 Laurence attended the funeral of James I as King's limner and retained this post under Charles I. But the last limning of James I, showing a much-aged figure, was not by the King's limner but by John Hoskins

(V&A). Laurence retained his court salary but effectively abandoned the role for which his father had prepared him. Instead Hoskins and his near contemporary Peter Oliver, son of Isaac, became the leading limners of the next generation.

Little is known about Hoskins' background. His earliest biography, by Bainbrigge Buckeridge, published in 1706 about 40 years after Hoskins died, states that he 'was a very eminent limner...bred a Face-painter in Oil, but afterwards taking to Miniature, he far exceeded what he did before'. The household accounts of Sir Hamon le Strange for 1617 confirm that two oil portraits of le Strange and his wife are by Hoskins. These portraits suggest that William Larkin may have taught Hoskins oil painting.[17] But no official record of an apprenticeship for the young Hoskins has yet been found. Most biographies of Hoskins state that the earliest miniatures known to be by him date from the early 1620s, but a miniature of an unknown woman signed 'IH' (Plate 35), overlooked by previous writers, has recently been dated to as early as 1615, when both Hilliard and Oliver were still working.[18] This miniature, with its Hilliardesque style and technique, begs the questions how and from whom Hoskins learnt this art.

One area of London has been identified as the principal home of limners or miniaturists: St Anne, Blackfriars, and the associated parish of St Bride, Fleet Street.[19] Isaac Oliver lived in Fleet Lane, towards Blackfriars, as did

Plate 35. John Hoskins, *Unknown Woman*, signed in gold, *c*.1615. Watercolour on vellum (49.5 x 39.5 mm). This modest miniature is an important early work by John Hoskins, who originally trained as an oil painter. With its red curtain background, use of gold and silver and overall jewel-like quality, it reflects the dominance of Hilliard's style at this time.
P.6-1942

Opposite: Plate 36. John Hoskins, *Lady d'Aubigny*, signed, late 1630s. Watercolour on vellum (84 x 67 mm). This work is a world away from the portrait of a woman painted by Hoskins over 15 years earlier in the Hilliardesque manner (Plate 35). This portrait of a lady at the court of Charles I shows the influence both of new fashions in dress and of Van Dyck's new portrait style.
P.105-1910

Plate 37 (actual size). Peter Oliver, *Tarquin and Lucretia*, c.1630.
Watercolour on vellum (114 x 99 mm). This is a copy after a picture in the
collection of Charles I and now in the Kunsthistoriches Museum, Vienna.
Royal records describe another version by the amateur limner, Sir James
Palmer, which in the 1630s was already in a bad state. This cabinet
miniature may have been a replacement. 1787-1869

Laurence Hilliard once he married in 1611, while Peter Oliver was a parishioner of St Anne. It is perhaps significant in terms of Hoskins' introduction to the limners area that his father was, for an unspecified reason, a prisoner in the nearby Fleet prison, and was buried in 1610 in the same church in which Laurence Hilliard's children were baptised. But while the young Hoskins probably lived among his fellow oil painters in another part of the city, both London and the circle of patrons for whom both sets of painters worked were too small for social or professional separation. For example, in 1613 William Larkin, who had possibly taught Hoskins oil, moved his workshop from the painters' area in Holborn to lodge near Isaac Oliver. Princess Elizabeth's impending marriage offered many opportunities to portraitists and Blackfriars, being on the river, offered ready access to her palace further downstream.[20]

While it is tempting to suggest that Hoskins was taught by Hilliard or Oliver, or even one of their sons, there were other limners. Nicholas Lockey, brother of Hilliard's apprentice Rowland, was involved in a court case at this time and although he was described as 'a citizen and Armourer of London' (the Armourers being his father's guild), the records state that he was 'useinge and professinge for his livinge...the arte of lymeinge... pictures'.[21] The examples of Nicholas Lockey, and possibly Hoskins himself (for whom there are no guild records), illustrate the breakdown in guild power and the way in which boys learned and practised one art, while official guild records tell a completely different story.

The Early History of the Cooper Brothers

Samuel Cooper and his brother Alexander were, according to Bainbrigge Buckeridge, 'bred up under the care and Discipline' of their uncle John Hoskins. But, like Hoskins, little is known of their history. It has recently been discovered that on 1 September 1607, a Richard Cowper married Barbara Hoskens, daughter of John Hoskens 'the prisoner in ye Fleett' in a church near the miniaturists' area of Blackfriars.[22] The evidence suggests that Samuel was their first child, born in 1608, and Alexander was born the following year. Their uncle was therefore only a little over ten years older than the boys; why and when they came to live with him is not known. However, Sandrart recorded in 1683 that Alexander was 'far-and-away Oliver's most famous pupil'.[23] Alexander clearly trained with Peter Oliver, while Samuel is known to have worked in Hoskins' studio. Both boys seem to have had a traditional apprenticeship, presumably from the age of 14. The work and careers of the two brothers were to follow very different paths, perhaps a reflection of the separate masters under whom they trained.

Peter Oliver and Alexander Cooper

Peter Oliver, unlike Hoskins, was brought up within the limning tradition. His early work is so like his father's, in whose studio he worked, that it is not always possible to distinguish the hands; Alexander Cooper's early work is similarly hard to distinguish from Oliver's. Oliver, like his father, worked for the children of James I, particularly Princess Elizabeth, whose husband became King of Bohemia (Plate 32) but was driven into exile. The couple became a European cause célèbre, and Elizabeth used portrait miniatures in the same propagandist fashion as her father. Alexander Cooper was probably introduced by Oliver to this prestigious circle based in the Netherlands at the Hague. By 1631 he seems to have been in the Netherlands, and although little is known of his movements, he was certainly in Sweden and Denmark; most of his work is found in foreign collections, particularly the Royal Collections of the Netherlands, Sweden and Denmark.

Alexander Cooper's internationalism seems to reflect Peter Oliver's Continental bias, that he in turn had inherited from his father. It is no surprise that Peter Oliver was the first limner in England to use professionally a gessoed card in place of a playing-card, an innovation of Balthazar Gerbier.[24] Gessoed card was a Continental drawing surface on which designs were scraped using metal point. But while such technical changes were of interest to other limners, patrons had different concerns. In 1625, the year that Charles I came to the throne, the king married a French princess, Henrietta Maria, who set a new standard of female fashion. This can be seen in Hoskins' *Lady d'Aubigny* (Plate 36): low-cut bodice with no ruff, simple pearl necklace and single pearl earrings, the hair clustered around the face in tight ringlets. This miniature does not just reflect a change in costume fashion, but also the new taste for the work of the oil painter Van Dyck who arrived in England in 1632.

Few portrait miniatures by Peter Oliver from the late 1620s are known, and it is possible that competition and demand after 1632 for Van Dyckian portraiture was not to Oliver's taste. Unlike his pupil, who sought markets abroad, Oliver concentrated on subject limnings, or as Norgate called them 'Histories in lymning', which he noted were 'strangers in England till of late yeares it pleased a most excellent King to command...some of his own peeces, of Titian...to be translated into English lymning, which indeed were admirably performed by his Servant, Mr Peter Olivier'. This idea was probably suggested by both Charles I's purchase of one of Isaac Oliver's unfinished 'histories', *The Entombment of Christ* (finished by Peter Oliver),[25] and by Sir James Palmer, the amateur limner, who is shown in royal records to have earlier copied one of the king's paintings, *Tarquin and Lucretia*, also copied by Oliver (Plate 37).[26]

John Hoskins, Van Dyck and Samuel Cooper

When Van Dyck came to work for Charles I in 1632 he was granted a house in the parish of St Anne, Blackfriars, where Peter Oliver had his workshop. The king, delighted with his new painter, paid for a 'a new cawsey Way...and a new paire of stares' leading from the waterside up into Van Dyck's garden, so he could go ashore from the royal barge 'to see his paintings'.[27] We do not know where Hoskins and Samuel Cooper lived at this time, but in 1698 Richard Graham wrote that Samuel Cooper benefited from 'the Observations which he made of the works of Van Dyck', and it is likely that, like Peter Oliver, they lived nearby. It is a striking fact that the first miniature with Cooper's own monogram is of Van Dyck's mistress, Margaret Lemon. Cooper was in his twenties when he painted this, but his earlier works are probably disguised under the monogram of his uncle 'IH'. The demand for miniatures was great and the variations in the miniatures bearing the 'IH' monogram suggest that Hoskins ran a workshop, probably with more assistants than just his nephew.

It is not easy to trace the specific development of Hoskins' art, but comparing Plate 35, painted around 1615, with Plate 36 from the late 1630s it is possible to identify more general changes in the appearance of miniatures between these dates. Firstly, Hoskins abandoned Hilliard's literal three-dimensional jewelling techniques, using instead a painterly two dimensional method to give the illusion of jewels, while silver and gold became less dominant. Henrietta Maria's simpler fashion probably helped to render Hilliard's techniques obsolete. The calligraphy and mottos that had disrupted the sense of the sitter occupying a real space had already begun to disappear with Hilliard's own replacement of the blue background with the red curtain. But Hoskins, no doubt in response to Van Dyck, introduced the dramatic innovation of the sky and landscape background (Plate 36). After 1632 Hoskins' miniatures unmistakably reflect the taste for Van Dyck's portraits.

Van Dyck's influence on Hoskins suggests that links between the two studios may have extended to Van Dyck's oils being moved to Hoskins' studio for copying. The pressure for such miniature versions undoubtedly came from the patrons who, even when they gave Hoskins an independent sitting, expected a Van Dyckian image. However, Hoskins' miniatures were not simply convenient, portable versions of Van Dyck's oils. Sir Kenelm Digby famously remarked that life-size portraits were 'so like as some people think them even the worse for it. The best faces are seldom satisfied with Van Dyck; whereas not the very worst even complained of Hoskins'.[28] The delicate precise technique of miniature painting at this date created a wholly different smooth effect, while the small size of the oval miniature inevitably softened the impact of imperfections that seem so overwhelming in a large-scale oil.

Settings and Uses of the Miniature

Today many miniatures from the sixteenth and seventeenth centuries are no longer in their original settings. Miniatures have been removed wholesale from their often precious gold or jewelled lockets. Lids have been removed, as have the pendants (the single pearl that hung from a loop at the base of a locket). Even in the eighteenth century original settings were uncommon. Horace Walpole recorded how 'a valuable treasure' of miniatures by Isaac and Peter Oliver (the latest dated 1633) was 'discovered in an old house in Wales that belonged to a descendent of Sir Kenelm Digby...Being inclosed in ivory and ebony case, and the whole collection locked up in a wainscot box, they are as perfectly preserved as if newly painted'. The number and variety are interesting: three of Digby himself; six of his wife, the famous beauty Venetia Stanley, at different ages; a large family group copied from Van Dyck; and a smaller version of the same, presumably rectangular which was 'set in gold richly inlaid with flowers in enamel and shut...like a book'.[29]

Venetia Stanley (Plate 38) was Digby's celebrated mistress and then wife, and many portraits of long-haired young women from the 1620s are described as being of her. The ivory case of this portrait gives an idea of what some of Walpole's 'treasures' might have looked like, although there would also have been a lid that preserved the miniature from fading in light. Ivory boxes had become a common setting for miniatures in the Elizabethan period (Plate 19), and in the early seventeenth century these were often stained black to imitate ebony; these seem to have gone out of fashion after the 1630s. From then onwards frames are usually simpler gold 'lockets' but often with no lid, although there is sometimes evidence of filing at the base of such frames, indicating that a lid has been removed (Plate 47). These frames are characterised by the scroll work at the top forming a loop to hang the work by (Plates 41 and 47). Nevertheless, simple lockets are still found (Plate 39) and plain ebonised fruitwood frames were also common, although the original seventeenth-century frame in Plate 40 is no longer with its original miniature.

Plate 38. Peter Oliver, *Unknown Woman*, probably Venetia Stanley, c.1615–17. Watercolour on vellum (67 x 54 mm). The fame of certain women, usually for their beauty and amorous liaisons, meant that their portraits proliferated much like images of royalty. Venetia Stanley, mistress and then wife of Sir Kenelm Digby was one such figure. P.3-1940

CHAPTER FOUR

FROM THE CIVIL WAR TO THE EARLY EIGHTEENTH CENTURY

Civil War

In 1634 Hoskins moved to the newly developed area of Covent Garden, which soon became the main artists' area in London. We know Cooper also moved with his uncle since that year Baron Theodore Turquet de Mayerne, doctor to Charles I, records visiting Hoskins to learn about the manufacture of pigments and Cooper jotted down one of his own recipes.[1] Such fleeting glimpses, however, are all we have of Cooper. His early biographers note fragments of information – that he was a renowned lutenist for example, and that he spent 'several years of his life abroad' which could simply have meant out of London. Certainly there are very few signed works from 1634 until 1642, when he finally set up independently in Covent Garden near his uncle, but we remain ignorant of why this should be.

The year Civil War broke out, 1642, was not an auspicious year to establish a business in London. Van Dyck had died the previous year, but had been organising his departure from an increasingly riotous city, and the king had finally abandoned London to set up court in York when his conflict with Parliament was approaching crisis. Cooper married some time before 1642 and a possible explanation of his movements at this time is suggested by the fact that his wife's family lived in York.[2]

The Civil War was in effect a prolonged series of riots, skirmishes, full-scale battles, negotiations, and broken promises stretching on until 1649 when the king was finally executed as a public enemy. Hoskins, who in 1640 had finally been granted an annuity by Charles I, only received one payment before events overtook demands on the royal purse. He died in straitened circumstances in 1664, leaving his widow to claim the arrears from the recently restored monarchy. Laurence Hilliard's son Brandon also petitioned Charles II for his father's unpaid salary, noting that his father and grandfather had 'faithfully served your Majesty's father, grandfather and ancestors', and that during the war Laurence had 'sustained many losses, imprisonments and troubles' for his loyalty.[3] Another limner, David des Granges, also petitioned the king for money in 1671. Des Granges, whose mother's maiden name was Hoskins, was clearly related to Hoskins and Cooper; the latter mentioned three 'degrange' children in his will. Des Granges left London in 1651 to act as limner to Charles II who had taken refuge in Scotland. The petition shows that Charles ordered a number of the portraits of himself that circulated after his father's execution; 13 such gifts to supporters are mentioned: 'one to Major Boswell who went to the Highlands, which your Majesty gave with your own hands'.[4] Peter Oliver, who had died two years before the king's execution, was spared having to choose between opportunities in London and loyalty to the king.

Samuel Cooper was not untouched personally by these years. The poet Alexander Pope, who was the nephew of Cooper's wife, Christina, wrote that she 'had three Brothers, one of whom was kill'd, another died in the service of King Charles'.[5] Professionally, however, Cooper flourished. Each resident in London was taxed for a 'Poor Rate' according to their income and in 1642 Cooper was assessed at six shillings, two shillings less than his uncle. Later, in 1650, Cooper was assessed at one pound, outstripping his uncle and exceeded only by three titled neighbours. Cooper's success was not a mark of his political loyalties. Artists, like most people, were pragmatic rather than ideological about the changes in power. In 1650 Peter Lely and Balthazar Gerbier planned a series of oils to celebrate the achievements of Parliament. Gerbier had previously worked for Charles I and Lely was to become the leading court painter under Charles II.

Cooper and Gibson during the Interregnum

From 1649 until 1653 England was subject to Army rule led by Oliver Cromwell, who from 1653 was officially styled as 'Lord Protector'. Cromwell and his family effectively took the place of the royal family and almost immediately required portraits for the same propagandist and diplomatic roles for which the monarchy had formerly used them. In 1656 it was agreed that £1500 would be spent on a gift to the Swedish ambassador consisting of cloth, a jewel and a miniature by Cooper.

The Cromwell family first employed Cooper as early as 1650, when Lord Conway, who wished to commission a portrait, received a note from Miles Woodshawe explaining, 'I spoke to Mr. Cooper, the painter, who desires you to excuse him one month longer, as he has some work to finish for Lord General Cromwell and his family'. It has recently been discovered that the portrait commission was for the niece of a Colonel Ashburnham. The portrait was delayed because Anne Ashburnham 'hath been very little in towne but after the holidayes are past shee will bee in towne and will then sitt'. A sitting to Cooper was clearly no quick matter, Cooper promising that once the lady was with him they would 'sitt a weeke together'.[6] When Pepys' wife Elizabeth sat to Cooper in 1668 the diarist records eight separate sittings, five more than Hilliard or Oliver would have required.

Cooper's leading competitor in London after the Restoration, Richard Gibson, lived and worked in an entirely different way during the Interregnum. Unlike Cooper, Gibson did not train within the highly competitive professional London art world. His early monogram 'DG', standing for the diminutive 'Dick' or even 'Dwarf', suggests the subservient role that Gibson, who stood at only three feet ten inches, initially adopted. In his twenties Gibson was a 'page' to Charles I, a position more usually associated with boys, while his marriage in 1640 was a celebrated court event, with the marriage register significantly recording that the couple were 'boethe Dowarfes'. Only later when he was independently established did he sign himself more confidently 'RG'.

Gibson learned drawing and limning under the patronage and encouragement of aristocratic patrons. By the

Plate 39. Unknown artist, *Charles II*, c.1644. Watercolour on vellum, signed G. I. (45 x 35 mm). Charles II became the focus for royalist sympathies after his father's execution, and numerous images of him were circulated. This miniature by an artist known only by his initials, is a copy of an oil painting by William Dobson. In its simple enamel locket it would have been a precious possession. E.442-1995

Plate 40. Richard Gibson, *Unknown Woman*, c.1657. Watercolour on vellum (74 x 60 mm).
This woman is likely to be of the close circle of aristocratic families for whom Gibson
worked during the Interregnum. P.15-1926

late 1630s he was attached to the household of Philip Herbert, Earl of Pembroke, who, as Lord Chamberlain, was one of the connoisseur collectors close to the king. Gibson was introduced to royal patronage and, like Peter Oliver, was employed painting copies of the king's collection; one of Oliver's copies after Titian was listed in royal records as being on loan to 'little Dick my Ld. Chamberleine's page to bee copied'.[7] When the king left London, Pembroke felt unable to take the king's part. He returned to his country seat, Wilton, and Gibson, without an independent practice, probably returned to his former patron's care. Pembroke died in 1649 but secured the future of his protégé, granting him an annuity. Gibson seems then to have moved to Ascot, the country seat of Pembroke's grandson Charles, second Earl of Carnarvon. After Pembroke's removal from London the family lived quietly away from the centre of politics. Gibson became the portrait painter to a group of patrons linked by family and political sympathy, temporarily suspended from government and political power but destined to return (Plate 40).

Limning after the Restoration

Cromwell's death in 1658, and the restoration of the monarchy in 1660, transformed London society. King Charles II, with his love of ease and pleasure, set a wholly different tone at court from that of the stern Cromwell. Exiles returned to London and Gibson's patrons were restored at court. Confident of the support of this newly powerful group, Gibson set up as a professional limner in London, while Cooper's reputation secured him the position of King's limner (Plate 42). It is a measure of the demand for Cooper's work, and of London's growth, that it took Samuel Pepys six years to meet Cooper, despite moving in similar circles. It was through Hayls, Cooper's cousin, who was painting Pepys and his wife, that Pepys met Cooper in a Covent Garden coffee house. Pepys visited Cooper's studio, and finally invited him, along with other artists and writers 'all eminent men in their way', to a mid-day dinner party.

When Cooper died in 1672 a number of leading miniaturists could have become King's limner: Gibson, Nicholas Dixon and another young limner, Peter Cross, whose portrait of Robert Kerr, fourth Earl of Lothian (Plate 44), shows the level of patronage he had already acquired. But no one limner had the pre-eminence of Cooper, and in time Gibson, Dixon and Cross were each

Plate 41. Samuel Cooper, *Sir William Palmer*, 1657. Watercolour on vellum (56.5 x 45 mm). Set in a gold locket, this miniature was clearly a cherished family possession, staying in the Palmer family until the 1950s. Palmer seems to have lived quietly through the Interregnum, although, like many men at this time, he is painted wearing his armour. P.3-1956

to receive royal appointments.[8] Competition in the field was increasing and other limners in London included des Granges, as well as semi-amateurs such as Thomas Flatman (Plate 46).

Cooper's Revolution of Style

If the seventeenth-century statistician Gregory King can be considered accurate, by 1680 two out of three English townsfolk lived in London.[9] With government, trade and industry centred on the metropolis, London dwarfed Paris. Cooper was the leading limner of his day, and commanded surprisingly high prices, but London had become too great a market to dominate as Hilliard had done. Cooper's work, however, was the standard against

Plate 42. Samuel Cooper, *James II* as Duke of York, 1661. Watercolour on vellum (80 x 64 mm). It is an indication of Cooper's reputation that James, Duke of York and brother of Charles II, immediately sought a sitting on the Restoration. This miniature could have commemorated James' return from exile or his secret marriage to Anne Hyde in 1660. P.45-1955

Opposite: Plate 43. Samuel Cooper, *Henrietta, Duchess of Orleans, c.* 1661. Watercolour on vellum (72 x 55 mm). The enlargement shows the bravura and freedom of Cooper's brushwork, particularly in the spring of the tight curls. P.110-1910

which others set themselves. He revolutionised attitudes to the handling of paint, using the brush with a boldness quite different from the neat, careful way in which Hilliard had modelled his portraits.

Other limners were inspired to develop equally individual ways of using the brush. Richard Gibson was possibly taught by the oil painter Peter Lely (Plate 49), and certainly his method is similar to that associated with oil. His portrait of an unknown woman (Plate 45), photographed with the light hitting it from the side rather than above (raking light), shows the roughness of his technique, like a thick dragged 'impasto' (paste-like pigment). Peter Cross could not have been more different in his approach. His portrait of Robert Kerr (Plate 44) has a wonderful soft-focus effect created by using delicate, soft touches and dots. It is a tonal technique with little sense of line, much like Isaac Oliver's *Head of Christ* painted 50 years earlier (Plate 3). While Oliver used blended touches of red and brown, Cross used separate colours such as red, blue, yellow and green that

Opposite: Plate 44. Peter Cross, *Robert Kerr*, fourth Earl of Lothian, 1667. Watercolour on vellum (75 x 63 mm). This virtuoso portrait shows Cross's wonderful soft-focus style created with delicate touches and dots. P.41-1981

Above: Plate 45. Richard Gibson, *Unknown Woman*. Watercolour on vellum (49 x 41 mm). This miniature has been photographed in raking light to show the rough surface created by Gibson's use of thick impasto. Evans 37

blend at a distance to produce smooth flesh tones. In contrast, the brushwork of Thomas Flatman is often thought of as dry and scratchy, and the overall effect unsympathetic and harsh. This has been seen as a possible failure of technique: the use of brushes that were too fine.[10] However, Flatman may have intended the effect deliberately to avoid smooth and blended brushwork and to draw attention to the techniques and materials – a form of honesty that opposed the vanity often associated with portraiture.[11] Flatman was also a lawyer and poet, and was not dependent on his art for a living, although his friend Charles Beale records paying him.[12] His portrait of Beale, husband of the artist Mary Beale and father of the limner Charles Beale Junior, is painted in this natural style; his three warts, not unsurprisingly, have neither been ignored nor disguised (Plate 46).

Problems of Attribution

The implication of such characteristic brushwork is that the work of each limner is easily identifiable. In fact, the process of attributing unsigned works has often been extremely difficult, because while the differences outlined above may remain evident, an artist's work nonetheless evolves over the years. The rough virtuosity of Cooper's early brushwork became more obviously

Plate 46. Thomas Flatman, *Charles Beale the Elder*, 1660 (previously thought to be 1664). Watercolour on vellum (82 x 70 mm). In Charles Beale's 'almanack' for 1661 he records: 'several wages to Mr Flatman for Limning my own picture'. Now that the miniature has been redated it is possible that this is the limning for which Flatman was paid. P.13 -1941

blended in his finished miniatures after the Restoration, a smoother technique that was more glamorous and flattering. It has been suggested that Cooper taught Nicholas Dixon, whose style in the 1670s shows the same fashionably high finish. At this time Dixon's miniatures were very distinctive, particularly those of women with their languorous air and almond-shaped eyes (Plate 47). This mood was wholly in tune with a court that took its lead from a king famed for his mistresses such as Nell Gwynn. Later, however, Dixon's works are rough and unfinished. Whether this change is a decline in stan-dards, or a deliberate attempt to create, like Flatman, a contrasting style to the easy glamour of his earlier court portraiture, is a subject of debate.[13]

Even signed works can present problems when there is little documentary evidence about the artists behind the monograms. For years 'DG' working roughly between 1640 and 1660, and 'RG' working from 1660 to the 1670s were thought to be two artists. Gibson's idiosyncratic style was the clue to a link between the two monograms. Similarly, for years it was thought that there were two separate artists, Lawrence Cross and Peter

Plate 47. Nicholas Dixon, *Unknown Woman*, c.1675. Watercolour on vellum (86 x 68 mm). Dixon was influenced by Cooper's work, blending his brushwork into a smooth finish. Dixon's works, however, are more formulaic, especially his portraits of women with their languorous almond-shaped eyes. P.4-1942

Cross. This was also a misinterpretation of a thoroughly misleading monogram of one artist, Peter Cross.

Sometimes problems of attribution have arisen because one artist assisted another artist. Such confusion occurred with Alexander Cooper (who worked with Peter Oliver) and with John Hoskins junior, and who seems to have helped his father through his last years as well as working independently, but with a monogram that was similar to his father's. Samuel Cooper also worked in Hoskins' studio into his twenties and almost certainly painted miniatures signed with the 'IH' mono-

gram. Cooper's own monogram has also presented problems, since unscrupulous restorers have sometimes added it to the work of other artists and, confusingly, to seemingly authentic but unsigned work by Cooper.

Copies, such as those by Susannah Penelope Rosse of Cooper's work, have also caused confusion. Rosse was only 17 when Cooper died, but grew up in the neighbouring parish and may have known Cooper through her father, Richard Gibson. 'Samuel Cooper's Pocket Book' as it was traditionally known (containing 14 seventeenth-century miniatures), initially confused the work

Plate 48a and b. (a) Samuel Cooper, *Unknown Woman* c.1660-65. Watercolour on vellum, laid on card with a prepared gesso back (96 x 70 mm). (b) Susannah Penelope Rosse, presumed self-portrait, inscribed on reverse 'Mrs Rosse', c.1685–90. Watercolour on vellum, laid on card with a prepared gesso back (93 x 71 mm). Two of 14 miniatures originally interleaved into 'Samuel Cooper's Pocket Book'. (a) 448-1892; (b) 457-1892

of these two artists (Plate 48). Four of the works are now agreed to be by Cooper and the rest, except one, by Rosse. Like most artists Cooper left a number of unfinished miniatures in his studio when he died, and these were eagerly sought after by collectors such as Charles II and Cosimo III. It is possible that the 'Pocket Book' of Cooper's belonged to the Rosses, since the sale of Michael Rosse's collection in 1723, over 20 years after Susannah's death, included original works by Cooper as well as acknowledged copies by Mrs Rosse.[14]

Despite the confusion caused by the 'Pocket Book', Rosse's own limnings do not imitate Cooper's style. They are a remarkably intimate record of her relations and neighbours, ranging from 1680 to 1690, including two possible self-portraits (Plate 48); her neighbour on

Henrietta Street, Mrs Pru Phillips; and her sister-in-law, Mrs Priestman. One portrait, supposedly of the Countess of Sussex, falls outside this intimate circle. Rosse was probably not a professional limner and a number of her portraits are obviously copies after other artists. She may have worked from prints and possibly had access to paintings through her cousin William Gibson, who acted as a picture dealer.

There are also unidentified limnings with a monogram, and limners who are documented as working at this time but to whom few miniatures have been attributed. What we know of the latter group, however, paints a fascinating picture of close neighbourly and familial relations. Matthew Snelling (according to Vertue 'a gentleman, who seldom painted unless for ladies with whom he was a mighty favourite and a gallant') was related to Mary Beale, the oil portraitist, whose husband Charles Beale was friends with Thomas Flatman (Plate 46). The Beales' son, also called Charles, undoubtedly learned limning from Flatman, but also sketched in Sir Peter Lely's studio (Plate 49) as did the limner William Gibson, and another shadowy limner called William Claret. Both Gibson and

Plate 49 (actual size). Charles Beale, after a self-portrait by Sir Peter Lely, 1679. Watercolour on
vellum (194 x 169 mm). Copying Old Masters was an established practice in limning.
This copy by Beale of a modern master, Lely, in whose studio he used to sketch, is a more
personal example of this practice. 555-1905

Figure 11 (actual size). David Loggan, *Unknown Man*. Plumbago (128 x 105 mm). Loggan was one of a number of artists, most of them printmakers, who introduced the Continental art of plumbago to England in the 1660s. P.18-1927

Claret belonged to the 'Virtuosi of St Luke' art club, founded in 1689.[15] Another member was Michael Rosse who lived with Susannah on Henrietta Street, where Samuel Cooper used to live, and near Peter Cross. Matthew Snelling, Nicholas Dixon and Cooper's cousin, the painter Hayls, lived nearby in Long Acre near to where Alexander Browne, who taught limning to Mrs Pepys, had his colourman's shop. The rarity of works by these artists has obscured the wider practice of limning at this date.

The Pressure of Competition

Most accounts of limning in Britain characterise the end of the seventeenth century as a period of decline. The majority of limners discussed above had died by 1700, or ceased to practise; only Peter Cross continued to work into the eighteenth century, dying in 1724.

The sense that one chapter had closed and another had

opened was encouraged by the replacement of vellum with ivory as the painting base, at the turn of the century. It is generally agreed that it was Rosalba Carriera (1675–1757)) who developed the technique of water-colour on ivory (Plate 50). Carriera became a renowned pastellist but originally was a decorator of snuff boxes, an essentially crude art which used watercolour but bore little resemblance to miniature painting. Her innovative 'fondelli' ('foundation' in Italian), little watercolour pictures on ivory, were painted with the soft powdery sophistication of her pastels. In 1705 her diploma piece, to secure her place as an Academician of the Academy of St Luke in Rome, was a self-portrait as 'Innocence', 'on an oval sheet of ivory rather less than a hand's breadth in size, glazed and fitted in a tin box'.[16] Two years later, Bernard Lens (1682–1740), painted the first miniature on ivory in England.[17]

The introduction of ivory seems to underline the declining fortunes of traditional limning in the last decades of the seventeenth century, in part the result of competition in the market for small portraits and the changing taste of patrons. David Loggan, who had trained abroad, came to England in 1658, becoming one of the earliest practitioners in England of plumbago (black lead) portraiture (fig.11). Graphite was actually the more usual medium for this delicate black-and-white portrait art, which originated in the print and book trades of the Netherlands in the late sixteenth century. Originally intended as preparatory drawings for prints, plumbagos also demonstrated a printmaker's graphic skill and became desirable in their own right. Working on vellum rather than the more perishable paper, print-makers such as Loggan offered works with the stature of limnings, at a lower cost. Plumbago was also more easily translatable into print, providing the client with almost exact reproductions.

A greater challenge to limning, however, was the enamel portrait (Plate 51). The French goldsmith Jean Petitot had introduced this recently perfected art to the court of Charles I. It was not until 1687, however, that the Swedish goldsmith Charles Boit reintroduced the art to England. Enamel gave Boit an entrée to the existing community of foreign artists, especially Michael Dahl, another Swede. On the Continent enamel was closely allied to oil painting as its vibrancy and shine made it a perfect medium for small reproductions of oil portraits, providing a client with two types of portrait from one sitting. Boit was further encouraged by William of Orange, husband of Mary (the daughter of James II), who in 1688 took the throne from the Catholic James at the invitation of leading Protestant aristocrats. William already knew Boit and created for him the position of 'enameller' at the court. As on the Continent, the enamel became established as an appropriate diplomatic gift.

Even in a simple setting, enamels have a rich jewel-like quality, and by comparison limnings seem low-key. The effects of light and damp on the delicate watercolour art were increasingly noted by those with ancestral limnings. Enamel, however, fired in a kiln after each application of pigment, was a tough, durable medium. Oval limnings had also become increasingly large and more suited to display in a cabinet than on the person, despite the cabi-net miniature of Sarah Churchill showing her wearing such a large limning on her wrist (Plate 52).

Durable enamels were also suited to being set either on the lid of, or hidden inside, snuff boxes (Plate 51). It is intriguing to consider whether the fashion for snuff

Plate 50 (actual size). Rosalba Carriera, inscribed on reverse by Horace Walpole: 'Robert, Lord Walpole, eldest son to Robert Walpole earl of Orford, drawn by Rosalba at venice. H.W.' Watercolour on ivory (84 x 59 mm). It was possibly through Grand Tourists such as Walpole that news of Rosalba Carriera's innovative technique of painting on ivory first reached England. P.160-1910

encouraged a taste for enamel, since many snuff boxes were enamelled. By the end of the seventeenth century snuff was a major social pastime, indeed habit, generating a huge market for the little boxes in which to carry this powdered tobacco. The box played an important part in the elegant ritual of taking snuff outlined in etiquette books. Occasionally the practice bordered on an obses-sion, with different boxes for every day of the week, or even year.

The fashion for enamel has sometimes been cited as a possible spur to the introduction of ivory – the employ-ment of one foreign novelty to challenge another. However, in 1707, the date of Lens' earliest miniature on ivory, Christian Friedrich Zincke (?1684–1767), whose enamel practice dominated the next few decades, had only just begun his training under Boit, while the long-established Peter Cross was still successfully practising limning. An advertisement in *The Daily Courant* (28 October 1707) asked for the whereabouts of a miniature, 'a lady's picture drawn in Watercolours…about 4 inches long set in a Princes Metal Case gilt', lost on its return to Cross from the goldsmiths. The most puzzling aspect of the use of ivory was that neither patron nor artist really gained any benefit from it. Ivory was a difficult working surface and the paint was often so thickly applied that the ivory would have not have been apparent to most observers.

A Wider Interest in Limning

By the turn of the eighteenth century, amateur practice of limning and the collecting of limnings had become significant aspects in the appreciation of the art. Interest in limning was not confined to commissioning a work from professionals such as Cross and Lens. Amateur interest especially must have affected perceptions of limning. On 7 May 1665 Samuel Pepys famously noted, 'Yesterday begun my wife to learn to limn of one Browne'. Alexander Browne was a writer and teacher of limning. In 1660 he published *The Whole Art of Drawing, Painting, Limning and Etching*, enlarged as *Ars Pictoria* (1669) and reprinted in 1675. Additionally he advertised himself as a colourman; 'because it is very difficult to procure the colours for limning rightly prepared', he had prepared a sufficient quantity to supply to others; furthermore, 'all other Materials useful for Limning, are to be had at my Lodging in Long-acre at the sign of the Pestle and Mortar'. A piece from Crowne's *Country Wit*, published the same year, illustrates the widespread assumption that gentlemen could limn: 'Merry: "Cannot you limn Sir?" Rambler: "Limne, what dost thou mean?" Merry: "Why limne, Sir, draw pictures in little."'[18] By 1712 Addison, writing in *The Spectator*, was sardonically noting: 'limning, one would think is no expensive Diversion, but…she paints fans for all her female acquaintance and draws all her relations pictures in miniature'.[19] Limning was clearly not seen solely as a professional art and one was as likely to be painted by one's sister as by a specialist limner. In his capacity as drawing master, Bernard Lens encouraged and benefited from this interest in limning. One such pupil was Princess Mary (daughter of George II), whose naive but attractive miniature on ivory of her sister was

Plate 52. Bernard Lens, *Sarah Churchill*, Duchess of Marlborough, wearing a miniature of her husband, 1720. Watercolour on vellum (401 x 266 mm). This miniature is undoubtedly a copy of an earlier oil painting, since in 1720 the sitter would have been 60 years old. It presents an interesting chance to contrast limnings which could be worn, and 'cabinet' miniatures.
627-1882

Opposite: Plate 51. Christian Friedrich Zincke (?1684–1767), *Sarah Churchill*, Duchess of Marlborough. Enamel (35 x 25 mm), set in a snuff box lid. Enamel was reintroduced to England at the end of the 17th century; its jewel-like brightness and durability offered an alternative to fragile limnings.

Figure 12. W. Humphry, after a drawing by George Vertue, *George Vertue and Margaret his wife in the very Habits they were Married; Feb 17th Anno domini 1720*. Engraving. Vertue was an engraver of antiquarian portraits, including miniatures. The display of small framed images was intended to represent his work and his interests. 22927

painted for her mother 'to wear in her snuff Box' (Royal Collection).

The families who could have afforded drawing masters such as Lens were also likely to have already had a small collection of ancestral miniatures. For many patrons a newly painted miniature would not simply be hidden away in a jewellery box, as a solitary example of the art. From such beginnings larger collections began to develop, and works with no family connection were bought. These could have been placed together in a cabinet, such as the one belonging to Horace Walpole (fig. 1), or displayed in a small room, also called a 'cabinet' (fig. 12). In 1743 the Prince of Wales' drawing room in Leicester House had the wainscot cut to 'receive 4 oval pannells with minnature pictures'.[20]

These collections benefited from, and were part of, a growing art world, the activities of which stretched beyond the artist's studio. In the late seventeenth century the many art institutions we have today did not exist, but were beginning to emerge. At this time independent dealers and one-off auctions both reflected and encouraged a growing interest in the collecting of art. Continental art, especially Italian, was the main focus of interest, as the Grand Tour became part of a young gentleman's education – travelling through Europe imbibing the culture and art, and often returning with a collection of so-called 'Old Masters'. However, the first

art appreciation club, the 'Virtuosi of St Luke', had, as discussed above, three members with a close interest in limning: Michael Rosse, William Gibson and William Claret. Another member, Richard Graham, wrote the first brief biography of Cooper and, like Rosse, held a significant sale of limnings. Interest in collecting limnings was as much a reflection of a growing interest in English history as aesthetic appreciation, as exemplified by Horace Walpole's collection of 'heads' (printed portraits of historical figures). The collecting of miniatures was bound up with the preservation and ordering of English history. Limners too became involved in the preservation of family collections and thus in the preservation of the history of their art. Peter Cross, who was himself a keen collector of miniatures, became an adviser and restorer. Most famously he was responsible for restoring a portrait, believed to be of Mary Queen of Scots, for the Duke of Hamilton. Cross restored the damaged miniature according to prevailing ideas of female beauty, which bore little resemblance to the queen's actual portrait (Plate 53).

The Miniatures of Bernard Lens

It is within this context that one should view Bernard Lens' work and career. Lens was the son of an engraver, also Bernard, who sometimes produced black-and-white portraits. His grandfather, another Bernard, was an 'enameller', though of what we do not know. Thus, his artistic roots are in practices effectively in competition with limning: namely, plumbago and enamel. Aged 14, Lens himself was registered for a goldsmith's apprenticeship in 1696, although he probably did not train as a goldsmith – by this time registration had become a way of establishing a right to practice in the City.

In 1697 his father and another engraver John Sturt set up the first commercial drawing school in England. One can imagine him leaving the leaflet advertising this 'Drawing School near the Hand and Pen in St Paul's Church Yard' in local coffee houses and taverns.[21] The innovation of Lens' father was modest compared to the larger 'academies' later established, but it set up Lens and his son as drawing masters. A letter written in 1707 to Robert Harley, father of Edward Harley (later the great miniature collector and patron of both Vertue and Lens), states, 'You was pleasd to desire me to speak to a person that could teach your son, Mr Edwd, to draw. I have sent for Mr Lens, a very able and the best master we have in London...His rate for teaching is a guinea entrance, and half-a-crown at time (for an hour's staying)'.[22] Though this could be the father, it was as a drawing master that Lens met his important patrons. Perhaps significantly, 1707 is the date of Lens' earliest-known miniature. It is possible that Lens was encouraged to paint on ivory by a pupil, or a pupil's relation, who had travelled in Italy and seen the innovative work of Rosalba Carriera or had sat to her (Plate 50).

Lens did not come from a limning background, but despite his seemingly radical work on ivory he became immersed in the limning tradition through the taste of his patrons, acting as a curator advising on collections and providing new frames to safeguard old pictures. These pearwood frames, stained black, are still called 'Lens Frames' and are found in many private collections today. Lens worked on vellum as well as ivory, with no apparent logic to his choice of base. He painted limned versions of the popular 'heads' produced in engravings by printmakers such as Vertue. But while he often used the appropriate vellum (Plate 54), many copies, such as the famous Mary Queen of Scots restored by Cross, are on ivory.

Lens also followed the seventeenth-century tradition of copying Old Masters in cabinet form, first seen in the work of Peter Oliver (Plate 37). These copies would have been specially commissioned by Lens' aristocratic patrons. Nicholas Dixon had ruined himself with an attempt to interest the open market in a taste that was the preserve of the elite, usually relating to their own collections of oil paintings. He was forced to mortgage 70 such limnings that he had no hope of selling individually.

Even some of Bernard Lens' straightforward portraits reflect his immersion in the art of the past. Plate 55 shows the sitter painted against the hard blue background last seen in Elizabethan miniatures. This portrait

Plate 53. Bernard Lens, in the style of, 'Mary Queen of Scots'. Watercolour on ivory set in a snuff box lid (59 x 73 mm). In the early 18th-century copies proliferated of two separate miniatures believed to be of Mary Queen of Scots, of which this is the most famous. (902-1882)

Plate 54a and b. Two copies of portraits from a series of English Heads of State. Watercolour on vellum. (a) *James I* after Nicholas Hilliard, by Bernard Lens; (b) *Oliver Cromwell* after Samuel Cooper, by Andrew Benjamin Lens (both dia. 50 mm). These miniatures were probably commissioned as an up-market version of the prints of the heads of historical figures, then in vogue with collectors. (a) E.594-1994; (b) E.599-1994

is one of 15 with similar backgrounds, recording the family of Richard Whitmore MP: his wife holding their baby; the other children holding a toy horse on wheels, a doll, a bow and arrow; and even a portrait of a baby wrapped in swaddling, painted lengthways on an ivory oval.[23] The other child in Plate 55 is a second cousin of the Whitmores, painted on a separate occasion.

It is easy to imagine Lens as a loner travelling from house to house, teaching, framing miniatures, making copies and painting family groups. However, in 1704 a new artists' club was established, 'The Rose and Crown'. Members included Lens, as well as Christian Frederick Zincke, George Vertue and William Hogarth.[24] A lost group portrait called *The Virtuosi of London*, painted in 1723 and now known only from a sketch, shows Lens in a convivial setting with his fellow artists. In 1711, 14 years after Bernard Lens senior's modest drawing school opened, an academy was established by the queen's prin-

Plate 55a and b. Bernard Lens, (a) *Richard Whitmore*, 1718. Watercolour on ivory (76 x 63 mm). (b) *Elisabeth Weld, c.1720.* Watercolour on ivory (74 x 62 mm). These two children are second cousins; both are painted on ivory, but the portrait of Richard has a blue background that deliberately refers back to Elizabethan miniatures. (a) P.13-1971; (b) P.65-1987

cipal painter, Sir Godfrey Kneller, open to all artists who could pay the subscription. 'The Rose and Crown' club had 85 members, half of whom, including Lens, also sketched at the academy. Lens was thus half in the old world of traditional limning for private patrons, and half in the modern artistic world in which large groups of artists would gather to draw, meet for a drink and discuss the latest ideas about art and business. Lens' work and career show that he was not partisan about the use of ivory or vellum – he was neither the conscious pioneer of a new medium, nor a backward-looking defender of past traditions.

CHAPTER FIVE

THE 1730S TO THE END OF THE EIGHTEENTH CENTURY

A New Era

A new century does not automatically proclaim a new era. As the last chapter discussed, despite the introduction of ivory in 1707 the first 20 years of the eighteenth century were a period of gentle transition, rather than revolution, in the history of English limning.

From the 1720s onwards, however, the character of English society became markedly different. A hint of these changes can be seen particularly in a new style of oil portraiture called 'conversation' pieces. These were small canvases depicting groups of figures taking tea, playing cards and music. These convivial groups are an age away from the solemn dignity of late seventeenth-century portraiture, showing men in heavy wigs with stern immobile faces and women in stiff poses, the only animation in their 'classical' drapes of silk.

The informal new style was popular even with the nobility. Vertue described a portrait in this style of Edward Harley, 2nd Earl of Oxford, by Gawen Hamilton, as 'family piece[s]…in the conversation manner…genteel and agreeable', but interestingly described conversations by another painter, Highmore, as 'pictures of citizens', 'family pieces…in the very habit they appear in', (meaning they were painted in the clothes and settings of their usual domestic life). People drew distinctions between a 'citizen' and a member of the nobility, but the conversation piece reflected a 'genteel and agreeable' age in which both could share in the country's increasing prosperity. In 1755 the French enameller André Rouquet, writing about the 'Present

Plate 56. Bernard Lens, detail from *Richard Whitmore* (Plate 55), 1718. Watercolour on ivory (76 x 63 mm). Lens' cautious stipple technique, to avoid the paint running on the ivory surface, is particularly noticeable in the face where careful individual dots are painted directly onto the bare ivory. P.13-1971

Plate 57. Jeremiah Meyer, detail of an *Unknown Man*, *c*.1780 (Plate 66). Watercolour on ivory (76 x 56 mm). Jeremiah Meyer was the first miniaturist to realise fully the potential of the difficult ivory surface, replacing cautious stippling with a bold virtuoso technique that did not allow for hesitancy or corrections.
Evans 167

that it was not transparent and many early miniatures were painted using the same thick layers of paint used on vellum. It was to be 40 years before English artists fully exploited the ivory support.

Lens produced miniatures the same size, and with the same dotted stipple, as the vellum miniatures by Peter Cross. But while Cross used stipple to create a soft focus effect (Plate 44), Lens' choice was one of necessity. On ivory, colour runs into puddles, and later strokes tend to 'pick up' earlier ones. Abandoning the traditional carnation, Lens painted the face in transparent colours straight onto the ivory using a cautious, mechanical stipple (Plate 56).

By the 1750s miniaturists had begun to improve both the ivory surface and their painting techniques. Ivory was cut more thinly, the saw marks removed by scraping, and the surface abraded with glass-paper and ground with wet pumice powder. Finally it was pressed between sheets of absorbent paper with an iron, and vinegar and garlic used to remove excess grease. The flow of paint

Figure 13. Miniature Painter's Box, 18th-century. This mahogany box is believed to have belonged to Richard Crosse (1742-1810). The frame has recently been fitted with a piece of ground glass on the assumption that it once contained some such material to diffuse the light. Below this is a little ledge for the ivory; the compact drawers would have contained colours, palettes and brushes. P.10-1925

State of the Arts in England' noted, 'it is amazing how fond the English are of having their pictures drawn but then peoples fortunes are more upon a level in England'. In 1756 the preface to Rolt's *New Dictionary of Trade and Commerce* summed up the defining characteristics of a new age: 'there was never...a time in which trade so much engaged the attention of mankind or commercial gain was sought with such general emulation'.

Miniature Painting on Ivory – Technical Developments

The miniatures from the mid-eighteenth century have been characterized as the 'Modest School', both for their unobtrusive size and the modesty of the period in which they were painted.[1] One likely reason for the size of these miniatures is that ivory was naturally oily and unabsorbent, and thus a difficult surface. Certainly, the idea that ivory replaced vellum because of its aesthetic effects is misleading. Initially ivory was so thickly cut

Plate 58a and b. (a) Luke Sullivan (1705–71), *Unknown Woman*, 1760. Watercolour on ivory (44 x 25 mm). (b) Nathaniel Hone, *Master Earle* aged 15, 1758. Watercolour on ivory (38 x 32 mm). For both these artists miniatures were only one aspect of their working lives. Luke Sullivan was an engraver and this beautiful miniature reflects the influence of rococo design. Nathaniel Hone was also an oil painter.
(a) P.30-1941; (b) P.4-1958

was improved, allowing greater freedom of handling, by the addition of more gum arabic. This resulted in greater transparency and artists began to exploit the pleasing effect of the luminous ivory showing through the paint.

Jeremiah Meyer was the first artist to realise fully the potential of these changes. Using the brush more adventurously, he created a graceful network of lines of varying length and colour. The bravura of this technique, allowing for no alterations, was quite unlike the hesitancy of Bernard Lens (Plate 57).[2]

With greater technical confidence, miniaturists soon developed distinctive styles. Many followed Meyer's linearism, such as Richard Cosway (Plates 61 and Frontispiece) and Richard Crosse (Plate 63). Others were more idiosyncratic, such as John Smart, who confidently used stipple to build up layers of gummy colour, creating an extraordinarily smooth effect; indeed, it is almost impossible to make out Smart's individual brush strokes except under magnification (Plate 62).

By the eighteenth century artists were spared the drudgery of preparing pigments by specialist shops selling cake watercolours, but essentially the materials and apparatus of miniature painting had changed little since the sixteenth century. Few new pigments had been invented, painting easels (fig. 13) were little different from that seen in Simon Benninck's self-portrait (Plate 9), and squirrel hair brushes were still used.[3]

The 'Modest School' and the Development of Ivory

Today's title of the Modest School obscures the fact that most of those who painted miniatures in the early eighteenth century would not have identified themselves primarily as miniature painters. The work of Thomas Frye, born in 1710, typifies the variety of activities undertaken by these artists, including oils, mezzotints, crayons, plumbagos, miniatures in watercolour, in enamel, and in oil. He was also manager of the Bow china factory. Consequently ivory miniatures by him are rare. Another artist, Luke Sullivan (Plate 58a), was born in 1705 and trained as an engraver, but he also painted landscapes and architectural views. Despite his obvious ability, ivory miniatures by him are again rare. Nathaniel Hone (Plate 58b), born in Dublin in 1718, came to England and worked as an itinerant portrait painter predominantly in oil but also in miniature.

Our understanding of this period is inevitably limited by our ignorance of many of the artists' lives. For instance, when Samuel Finney (1718–1798) first came to London in 1748 he noted only two competitors, Gervase Spencer and an artist he so disliked that, with the decorum of the age, his memoirs note him only as 'T'.[4] Clearly, in the eyes of Finney, 'T' was a leading miniature painter, but today he is unidentifiable. It seems, however, that most of these artists learned miniature painting as amateurs. Penelope Carwardine, whose father financially ruined the family, earned her living by this genteel art and by 1750 was an established miniaturist in London. The former footman Gervase Spencer was self-taught – his first miniatures date from 1740 – as were Samuel Finney and Samuel Collins who both trained as attorneys. Significantly, Samuel Cotes was trained as an apothecary like his father, while his elder brother Francis was apprenticed to the pastellist George Knapton; Francis Cotes subsequently taught painting to his younger brother.

None of these artists learned miniature painting as an apprentice under a master. Interestingly, R. Campbell's *The London Tradesman* (1747), which advised parents of suitable apprenticeships, included fan painting and oil painting, but not miniature. In contrast Charles Boit was apprenticed as a goldsmith from 1677 to 1682 and then learned enamelling as an extension of this training, and in turn taught enamelling to another goldsmith Christian Friedrich Zincke. Zincke's most noted student was Jeremiah Meyer, the son of a portrait painter. In 1757 at the substantial cost of £200, with an additional £200 for materials, the 14-year-old Meyer was placed by his father to learn this difficult art. It was not until 1760 that miniature painting acquired a sufficiently professional profile to prompt the mother of Ozias Humphry to apprentice him, at a cost of £100 for three years, to Samuel Collins, the former attorney.

Traditions and techniques were usually passed on under a master/apprentice system but, by becoming an art in which most practitioners were self-taught, these links had been broken. Samuel Finney, for example, as his memoirs and letters show, was wholly unaware of limning's history and of the fact that ivory was a recent innovation. The artists of the Modest School worked individually to resolve the technical difficulties of working on ivory, but the growing sophistication of the miniatures also reflects their involvement in a wider artistic practice. Luke Sullivan's miniature of a young woman (Plate 58) shows the influence of the Huguenot emigré engravers in its rococo freedom and movement.

Samuel Finney

Samuel Finney began to paint miniatures around 1748 and retired in 1768, just before the establishment of the Royal Academy. His memoirs, written in the third person, and his letters offer an insight into a frequently neglected period. His account explains how he introduced himself to the public, established his reputation, and carved out a career in the years before exhibitions of art gave artists easy access to the public.

The Beginnings of Finney's Miniature Practice

Finney took up miniature painting having become disillusioned with law. Spending a vacation with his uncle in Wales he indulged in his 'favourite amusement, Drawing', and, thinking that he 'might attempt a head from life', persuaded his uncle to sit for a portrait in indian ink. His efforts were so admired that others asked for their picture, earning Finney enough money in three months to return to London. He took lodgings in the Strand, and on showing his ink drawings to acquaintances was encouraged to try miniatures. Finney 'fell greedily to Work in practising upon Ivory with Water colours in which he soon acquired skill enough to entitle him to three guineas a head'.

Invited by a friend, Mr Legh, to travel to Bath together where Legh would 'recommend and introduce him into Business', Finney noted that 'most young Artists made their first campaign in one of the polite watering places'. The support of influential friends could make all the difference to an artist's career. When Finney tried his luck in Bristol he 'procured Friends' and received an invitation to stay at Lord Aston's country seat 'to paint him some pictures there'. 'This proved afterwards a good connection', introducing Finney to other wealthy patrons.

In addition to such personal recommendations, an artist could also advertise. In Bath Finney had 'declared his profession' in the *Bath Journal* of 25 April 1748: 'Miniature Painter in Water-Colours. Lodges at Mr Bush's, Apothecary, near the Abbey-Green in Bath, and begs leave to inform the Gentlemen and Ladies, that he takes Faces at Three Guineas apiece, and hopes to make his Performance agreeable to such as please to honour him with their Commands'. Finney also tried to ingratiate himself into society by going to places such as the Assembly Room, where concerts and dances were held, and the Pump Rooms, where people socialised and took the waters of Bath. Unfortunately, he had timed his arrival in Bath too late for the 'season', as the wealthy potential patrons who briefly descended on the town were moving on to London. In later years an artist could exhibit his self-portrait at a public exhibition to introduce himself and his work to potential patrons.

Returning to London, Finney 'fell to work again losing no time either painting portraits from the Life or copying good miniatures' with which his friends supplied him, 'by which means he improved everyday in the Art and begun to be taken notice of'. At this date, 1748, Finney could have subscribed, like fellow artists such as William Hogarth, to the St Martin's Lane Academy to improve his drawing by working from the life model,[5] but instead he chose to perfect his watercolour technique. In Finney's estimation he had only two rivals in London, and he therefore found examples of their work to copy. For Finney, as a self-taught artist, copying was an important part of his training. When staying with his friend Legh he had copied 'some good pictures there'.

Finney's Portrait Business

Displaying his business acumen in his choice of setting for his portrait practice, and 'incommoded by the Noise of the Neighbours Braziers shop' – not the atmosphere in which to advance one's reputation – he moved to share a building with the oil painter Edward Penny in the newly fashionable Leicester Fields. Situated near the town houses of the rich and landed, he 'was now conveniently and creditably situated encreasing in his reputation and his business every day'.

Careful with the finances of his portrait business,

Finney noted advances in his earnings and the advantages they could buy. In 1758 his rent was £40 a year while he was making £200 to £300 a year. The Finneys were therefore able to afford summer lodgings at Richmond and, in addition to their maid, employed a man servant in livery to greet sitters. André Rouquet's book of 1755, *The Present State of the Arts in England*, noted that: 'Every portrait painter in England has a room to shew his picture...People who have nothing to do, make it one of their morning amusements, to go and see these collections. They are introduced by a footman without disturbing the master'. The curious often came to gossip about the sitters and Finney himself records an occasion when some visitors were particularly unflattering about the queen, calling her 'a pug' (Plate 59).

Finney and his Competitors

Finney complained that miniatures 'did not afford the same opportunities of getting a Fortune as the painting portraits as large as life' because miniaturists worked alone, while an oil painter employed others for backgrounds and drapery, paying very little and so making a 'handsome profit'. Intriguingly, in 1763 Finney briefly employed 'a young Miniature painter to do his backgrounds and Draperies...to hasten his work', but he found it took him so long to unite and harmonise the separate parts that he returned to painting alone.

Although Finney's earnings increased from £200 in 1758 to about 500 guineas in 1763, he was acutely worried by growing competition. The Society of Artists held its first public exhibitions in 1760, and Finney noted in his memoirs for 1763 that 'last year observing the great Exercise of the Artists in the Water colours Miniature Branch he was apprehensive of some ingenious rival starting up'. The next generation of miniaturists, Cosway, Smart, Crosse and Humphry were all in their early twenties at this time and exhibiting at the Society of Artists.

Concerned for his watercolour practice, Finney decided to learn enamel painting. Like his main rival Gervase Spencer (Plate 60) he resolved 'to attempt this difficult Art too without a Master and after much study, many Experiments, Inquirys, disappointments and great Expences...finished an Enamel Portrait'. Enamel was a difficult medium, carrying risks of cracking when firing each layer of pigment. Finney painted many enamels, 'some bad some tollerable and a few good,' and believed

Plate 59. Samuel Finney, *Queen Charlotte*, after Allan Ramsey, 1760. Watercolour on ivory (46 x 39 mm). This portrait is after the coronation portrait by Ramsay, rather than one of the many works from life Finney painted for the young queen.
Evans 114

that his reputation in the distant future depended on those 'few' enamels because 'little Durability was to be expected from his deceitful water colour performances'.

It is ironic that in the same year that Finney took up enamel, 1763, the new young queen from Germany decided to appoint Finney her 'miniature painter' at a salary of £50 a year. However, her courtiers could find no precedent for this title. They were unaware of the older title of 'limner' that had fallen into disuse once Charles Boit had been appointed enameller under William III – the limner Bernard Lens had been appointed 'enameller' to the king. Finney was the first Royal appointment under the new term Miniature Painter.

Along with Spencer, Finney established watercolour miniatures as a profession in which young artists felt tempted to train. Through the pre-eminence of this generation of watercolour miniaturists, and the renewed vibrancy of miniature, enamel began to go out of fashion. Even Finney's hated rival, 'that Rascal Miers', Jeremiah Meyer, who had trained in enamel at great expense, took up watercolour miniatures, becoming one of its virtuoso performers. Finney however, having made his fortune and fearing the growing competition, retired in 1768 to the country, the year the Royal Academy was founded.

Settings and Uses for Finney's Miniatures

Enamel was a 'difficult' art and Finney charged 12 guineas for an enamel and six guineas for miniatures. Finney's patrons, however, do not seem to have commissioned watercolour or enamel with any sense that one was more desirable than the other. Indeed, once Finney

Plate 60a and b. Gervase Spencer: (a) *Unknown Woman in Turkish Costume*, 1757.
Enamel (48 x 41 mm). (b) *Unknown Woman*, 1749. Watercolour on ivory (64 x 46 mm).
These portraits illustrate the differences in strength of colouring between enamel
and miniature. Neither work is in an original frame.
(a) P.4-1943; (b) 194-1904

began to offer both, patrons often asked for the same portrait in both media. Colonel Graeme, who introduced Finney to the queen, asked for two miniatures of the queen's first sitting with Finney, 'one in enamel to be set with jewels to wear in a scotch bonnet for his own appearance at a Ball'. Finney arranged for miniatures to be set for his patrons. In a letter to his wife from Manchester he wrote that he was sending a parcel of three pictures, 'two of them are of the same size, Mr lever's and his mother Lady Lever. These are to be set in gold, plain, for Braclets; the other which is the largest is Mrs Lever and that is to be set in gold also as to hang to a watch'. The last miniature, intended to be worn like a watch on a chain, was also to have a 'fishskin case to fit it when set'. The Levers apparently wanted these miniatures in time to wear them to the Races. Finney clearly worked in a variety of sizes and in another letter from Manchester warned he was sending another picture 'to get set for a Ring'.

The Beginning of a New Era in Miniature Painting

In 1763, *Mortimers Universal Director*, an early trade directory, listed over 15 artists who advertised as miniature or enamel painters. Samuel Finney was included, but three names heralded a new era in miniature painting: John Smart, who advertised himself as a miniature painter, and Richard Cosway and Richard Crosse who advertised as 'Portrait Painters'.[6] One name missing from this group is Ozias Humphry, who by 1763 was working as a miniature painter in Bath.

Samuel Finney noted in 1767 that 'two or three formidable competitors in [my] line had lately started up'. He felt that he maintained his 'preheminance in the opinion of the Town', but was concerned that 'the polite Arts were now making a rapid progress' and that 'the publick in a few years would acquire a Corrector Taste and expect better Drawings than his'. Finney's competitors had, in contrast to his amateur background, been 'regularly bred to the profession', with training in drawing that he felt he lacked.

The artistic backgrounds of Cosway, Smart, Crosse and Humphry were entirely different from that of the Modest School and almost identical to each other. They were all born in about 1742 outside London: Cosway, Humphry and Crosse in Devon, and Smart in Norfolk. In 1754 a group of influential men, including the drawing master William Shipley, met to discuss an idea to encourage industry by offering prizes drawn from a fund contributed by public-spirited people; as the minutes of this meeting record: 'It was likewise proposed, to consider of giving rewards for the Encouragement of boys and girls, in the Art of Drawing...ye Art of Drawing is absolutely necessary in many employments, Trades, and Manufactures'.[7] A prize of £15 was offered for the best drawings by children under 14, and children between 14 and 17, and an advertisement to this effect soon appeared in the *Daily Advertiser*. Cosway, Smart and Crosse all won prizes, though Humphry clearly missed the Society of Arts advertisement. However his mother saw another advertisement in the local Barnstaple newspaper for William Shipley's drawing school in London.[8] Mrs Humphry, a lace maker, took a utilitarian view of drawing. Ozias was dispatched to London to learn drawing, to make contacts with lace makers and to provide her with new patterns. Humphry

Plate 61 (actual size). Richard Cosway, *Mrs Lowther*, c.1780. Watercolour on ivory (44 x 36 mm), set in the lid of an ivory and gold piqué snuff box. The sitter, artist and possibly the eventual owner of the miniature clearly intended a very different appearance from more conventional portraits. Cosway had earned a reputation for semi-erotic miniatures which developed from his early 'fancy' miniatures for snuff boxes. P.101-1931

Plate 62. John Smart (1742–1811), *Self-Portrait*, 1797. Watercolour on ivory (87 x 70 mm). Royal Academy records for the common name of 'John Smart' are unreliable, but this self-portrait, dated 1797, was probably exhibited that year at the Academy since this was the date of his first appearance there. P.11-1940

Plate 63 (actual size). Richard Crosse, *Mrs Siddons*, 1783.
Watercolour on ivory (174 x 133 mm). Portraits of the famous, such as
the actress Mrs Siddons, were often painted to be exhibited and
then kept in the studio to impress potential sitters. P.146-1929

lodged with family friends, and joined Smart, Cosway and Crosse, who had also been placed at Shipley's. This was not an apprenticeship but a training in drawing, 'heads, figures, flowers &c', at a cost of half a guinea entrance and one guinea a month for two days a week. In a letter to his mother Humphry defends his drawing of heads (rather than lace patterns), adding that 'there are many people who get a very handsome livelihood at it'. Mrs Humphry evidently came to consider miniature a suitable trade and her son was apprenticed to Samuel Collins. The Humphrys had only paid the first £50 of the fee before Collins absconded to Ireland in debt. A judge officially excused Humphry from his three-year apprenticeship and Humphry inherited the practice. We do not know if Cosway received a formal training in miniature. His first dated miniature is from 1760, and it is known that he was 'employed to make drawings of heads for the shops, as well as fancy miniatures and free subjects for snuff-boxes for the jewellers, mostly from ladies he knew'.[9]

In 1758 Shipley wrote to Humphry in Bath with news of 'greater opportunities of perfecting your studies' in London, 'for the Duke of Richmond has opened an Academy, which is filled with casts of the most capital of the antique statues'. These could be studied free of charge by students 'properly recommended', and 'Masters were also provided to...correct the labours of the student'. Here, it was hoped, the young student would learn to aspire to create great art.

The Society of Artists and the Royal Academy

The next developments in the art world were built on such dreams. Ever since Bainbrigge Buckeridge wrote 'Towards an English School' in 1706, discussion among artists and art lovers had centred on the foundation of an institution to promote English artists. In 1760 the first exhibiting society was established which, as Francis Hayman the painter put it, was 'a public receptacle to contain the work of artists for the general advantage and glory of the nation'.[10] There were concerns about who the 'public' would be, and efforts were made to exclude 'improper' persons 'such as livery servants, foot soldiers, porters, women with children, etc.' Despite artists complaining of 'the intrusion of persons whose stations and educations disqualified them for judging of statuary and painting', the exhibition was an enormous success.[11] Some participants however wanted not just an exhibition

Figure 14. P. A. Martini after H. Rambert, detail of an engraving of the 1787 exhibition at the Royal Academy. The first exhibition held by the Royal Academy in 1769 had only 139 exhibits, growing to around 1194 objects in 1797. The 'Miniatures' section was arranged around the fireplace in the Great Room. 27807

space, but to elevate English art by instilling the next generation with higher aspirations. In 1768 this faction, led by Sir Joshua Reynolds, established the Royal Academy with the approval of King George III. In addition to an exhibition space there was a school to train boys in the art of drawing, especially from life. Such academic training in the human nude was the bedrock of history painting, and this art of grand and morally elevating narratives of classical history would, the Academicians believed, bring credit to England.

Patronage, Ambition and Virtuoso Pieces.

These ambitions influenced the work of many artists who showed at the first exhibitions. Away from their private studios, miniaturists for the first time placed their work alongside not just other miniatures but oil

Plate 64 (actual size). Samuel Cotes, *Mrs Yates in the role of 'Electra'* in Voltaire's 'Orestes', 1769. Watercolour on ivory (152 x 127 mm). This miniature of an actress emulates Joshua Reynolds' grand portraiture, where ladies were portrayed as classical figures. P.1-1951

Plate 65 (actual size). Richard Cosway, *Sarah Bunbury*, later Lady Sarah Napier, *c*.1765–70. Watercolour on ivory (52 x 45 mm). This is a rare example of an early miniature by Cosway, showing the influence of Reynolds' oils. His later miniatures avoided such compositional complexity and heavy colouring. P.64-1935

Plate 66 (actual size). Jeremiah Meyer, *Unknown Man*, *c*.1780. Watercolour on ivory (76 x 56 mm). Meyer developed a linear style of painting (see Plate 57), which inspired Cosway (Frontispiece), Crosse (Plate 63) and others. Like all leading miniature painters of his generation, Meyer's early works were small, but with growing technical confidence the size of the ivory increased to an average of three inches. Evans 167

STRIKING LIKENESSES

Are taken by *A. R. BURT*, at *Mr. Gooch's, Bookseller,*

113, *HIGH-St.*

TERMS.

	£. s. d.		£. s. d.
Coloured Profiles . . .	10 6	Sketches of the Full Face .	1 1 0
Half Length	1 11 6	Full Length	2 2 0

Likenesses in Cameo, carved on Shell . . £3 3s.

Miniatures on Ivory, 3, 5, and 10 Guineas each.

☞ *The Public are requested to inspect the Specimens in Mr. BURT'S Painting Room.*

Figure 16. Facsimile reproduction of a trade card for Albin Roberts Burt (1783–1842) *c.*1803. In an increasingly crowded market few artists painted only miniatures. Burt's sitters could choose from 'Coloured Profiles, Sketches of the full face, half length, full length, likenesses in cameo, carved on shell, miniatures on ivory'.

paintings. The exhibitions were in part a trade fair: the artists demonstrating to the public what they might commission themselves (fig. 14). However, grouped with fellow artists, there was not only a need to stand out to catch the public's eye, but the desire to impress one's colleagues. Self-portraits, such as that by John Smart (Plate 62), served both to publicise an artist and to demonstrate technical skill. Richard Crosse often produced exceptionally large pieces for exhibitions and, like many artists, would seek to attract the public's attention by displaying portraits of famous figures. Portraits of actors and actresses, like his *Mrs Siddons*, (Plate 63), were particularly popular.

Although such pieces were invariably painted at the artist's expense, buyers could be found. Early in Humphry's career, George III bought a portrait of the St Martin's Lane Academy porter and life model, John Mealing, for 100 guineas at the Society of Artists. Humphry proudly asserted its 'superiority over all the surrounding examples of his contemporaries'.[12] However, for an uncommissioned miniature to be bought was rare. In 1782 Samuel Shelley, ahead of his time, exhibited a scene from Shakespeare entitled *Macbeth and the Witches* (V&A). When Shelley died, 70 such 'historical' pieces remained in his studio. Often such virtuoso pieces would remain with the artist, not as works that failed to sell, but as a 'gallery' for sitters to peruse.

The Influence of Reynolds on Miniature Portraits

The work of some miniaturists became grander, influenced by tastes in oil painting. Sir Joshua Reynolds had developed a form of portraiture based on classical art: his male sitters adopted poses of classical statues, while women were dressed as classical subjects. Two miniatures in the V&A by James Scouler, of two women, one as a 'Sibyl' and the other as the goddess 'Diana', reflect this taste. Samuel Cotes' portrait of Mrs Yates as 'Electra' (Plate 64), exhibited at the first Royal Academy Exhibition in 1769, also owes much to this grand idea of portraiture. Only a decade before, Cotes, like many of his colleagues, had been painting elegant miniatures measuring one inch, showing only the head and shoulders. 'Electra', however, measures six inches and this presented Cotes with many technical problems, aside from managing a complicated composition. Techniques for painting the costume and background, which on a small ivory produced barely noticeable areas of matt paint, were both obvious and unattractive on a large ivory. In contrast Crosse's *Mrs Siddons,* painted more than 15 years later, exploited the technical advances made by Jeremiah Meyer (see Plates 57 and 66) and used the ivory as an element rather than a problem. The resulting luminosity seems to justify the choice of ivory as a base, made over 70 years earlier.

Figure 15. Detail of an engraving of *The Royal Academicians in the Life Class*, by Richard Earlom after Johann Zoffany RA. The life class provided an appropriate setting for a portrait of the Academicians. Richard Cosway (lower right) strikes the pose of the Apollo Belvedere, exhibiting the ego that made this tiny man a butt of cartoonists' jokes. 24678

During the early years of the exhibiting societies young miniaturists were experimenting and developing their own distinctive styles. *Sarah Bunbury* (Plate 65) is an interesting example of an early work by Richard Cosway (showing the influence of Reynolds), painted in the 1760s before he developed his very different mature style.[13] Samuel Shelley, however, never deviated from his early admiration for Reynolds, and his style and technique emulated the composition and forceful colouring of Reynolds' oils (Plate 67).

The 'Disgrace' of Miniature Painting

Ozias Humphry felt that the art of the miniaturist was not an honourable pursuit: 'you know what excesses one is tempted to from a desire to excell in one's art, for I am sure a love of money never would have tempted me, but if it be a sin to covet honour, I am the most offending soul alive'. Following in the footsteps of his role-model, Sir Joshua Reynolds, Humphry travelled to Italy, eager to 'make one more effort, if I die for it', to paint large commissions. 'I feel very little disposed to adopt minia-

ture painting for life. I could not live under the disgrace of it', he wrote, although this was how he funded his stay in Italy, with great success.

In the 1760s Finney had shown some anxiety about a rising generation of artists who 'criticised the Drawing of everything in his pictures except the head which they all allowed as good as the best of them'. Humphry similarly criticised his friend Richard Collins, 'a miniature painter of great merit' but whose merit was 'wholly confined (like Samuel Cooper) to the circumference of a head', because he had not developed his 'inventive faculties' through 'academical practice after the human figure'. In thrall to the reputation of Reynolds, whose inventiveness was stimulated by such academic study, Humphry resented fellow miniaturists for not attempting to raise the reputation of an art to which he felt relegated. But Collins, who had attended life classes at the Academy, chose to paint traditional unpretentious miniatures and would probably have found his friend's criticisms amusing. Miniature painting was still hugely popular with the public whose main concern was to have a good likeness, and numerous artists offered this service (fig. 16).

Plate 67. Samuel Shelley, *The Misses Annabella and Mary Crawford*, 1782.
Watercolour on ivory (81 x 65 mm). Shelley was one of a number of
miniaturists influenced by Joshua Reynolds, imitating both the complexity of
composition and the rich colours of oil portraits. P.7-1925

However, sentiments similar to Humphry's would spur Andrew Robertson, early in the next century, to take miniature painting in a different direction.

New Markets for Miniatures

Many young artists flocked to London in the hope of acquiring fame among their peers at the Royal Academy or the patronage of Royalty, but London was not the limits of the market. In the early eighteenth century places such as Bath and Wells had offered artists a 'season' in which to paint the gentry before they returned to their country houses or to London. Towards the end of the eighteenth century the increase in trade, together with the beginnings of the Industrial Revolution, brought prosperity to numerous English towns, many of which developed their own art societies. In Ireland, the Dublin Society was founded as early as 1731; by 1740 Dublin had its own drawing school and in 1765 the Society of Artists of Ireland held its first exhibition. Surprisingly, such institutions did not appear in Scotland until the early nineteenth century, and Scottish artists travelled to London for training and encouragement. In Liverpool, Thomas Hazelhurst (Plate 68) found enough sitters for a lifetime's work, and his records show that he made over £20,000.[14]

The Challenge of America

While Samuel Finney was becoming established in London in 1750 he wrote to his father, who lived in Philadelphia, America, to ask if he could visit, enquiring

Plate 68a and b. (a) Richard Cosway, *Unknown Boy*, 1799. Watercolour on ivory (89 x 68 mm).
(b) Thomas Hazelhurst, *The Rt Honourable J. A. Plantagenet Stewart, c.*1800. Watercolour on
ivory (76 x 63 mm). Only a year apart in date these miniatures show two boys whose parents
had very different ideas of children's fashion. The London-based Cosway was the most
fashionable miniaturist of his day, while Hazelhurst had a flourishing practice in Liverpool,
profiting from the industrial boom. (a) P.7-1941, (b) Evans 133

if he could fund the journey by painting during his stay. His father wrote in reply that painting was 'a genteel [profession] and very profitable to such whose inclination lead'em to travel through the polite parts of our English America'. He had noted 'some Gentlemen of that profession in these parts', but 'whether painting in miniature wou'd be so well succeed I really can't tell'. Perhaps if his son could paint in oil, copying 'religious nightpieces, crucifixions…and the like' he would do well, 'for there's a great many roman Catholics in Philadelphia'. The idea of launching oneself into such uncharted territory probably did not appeal, especially since Finney's career in London became very successful. However, for the next generation of artists the trials of an increasingly crowded market enhanced the appeal of finding work in Britain's burgeoning Empire.

In 1776 America won independence from Britain, but began to attract an increasing number of British miniaturists. By moving to America an artist usually intended to make a new life, so reasons other than the pressure of the market place or thwarted ambition inevitably came into play, although these reasons are not always known. Edward Miles, who had exhibited at the Royal Academy for 22 years, moved first to Russia, working for the Czar for six years, and then at the late age of 55 settled in Philadelphia, in 1807, where he lived and worked until his death in 1828. Others committed themselves to a new life at a younger age. Archibald Robertson, brother of Andrew Robertson (Plate 73) was originally from Aberdeen; having spent five years in London he moved at the age of 26 to New York. His other brother Alexander joined him in 1792 and together they estab-

Plate 69. John Smart, *Unknown Indian Gentleman*, 1789. Watercolour on ivory (55 x 44 mm). Despite the tiny compass of this miniature, Smart's idiosyncratic style powerfully communicates the character of this gentleman. Smart worked successfully in India from 1785–95. P.16-1984

lished the Columbian Academy, which for a time was on Liberty Street. As well as his teaching, he wrote a treatise on miniature painting, painted portraits, miniatures and executed 'devices in hair work for lockets' (see Plate 78); examples of his work are found in America today. Many such artists not only encouraged a taste for miniature paintings, but taught others the art while contributing to the wider development of art in America.

The Opportunities of India

In contrast, India in the late eighteenth century offered the lure of monetary opportunity rather than that of a new life. In the early eighteenth century there were fewer than 1500 English people in India (mostly representatives of the East India Company, a trading company granted its charter in 1600 by Elizabeth I). The English crown had never taken a direct role in India, but in the 1750s the war with France spilled over into their respective concerns in India. The fight for influence in the area left the East India Company (designed for commerce) effectively representing England, wielding imperial power, imposing taxes and administering justice, resulting in massive profits for Company members. India became 'an El Dorado for young men in search of a fortune'[15] in the late eighteenth century. There was a huge growth in the expatriate community as members returning with their riches encouraged others to try their luck. This large community, stranded from home and loved ones, attracted many artists such as Ozias Humphry and John Smart seeking their fortune. In a letter to his brother, Humphry quoted the example of a painter in his street who had made '£30,000 in eight years'. He despaired of making a fortune in London and was also tired of 'the continual mortification of insignificance'. Having heard that there was no 'tolerable miniature painter' in India he resolved to go. The East India Company granted him permission to travel and to paint miniatures on the boat to cover his costs. However, Humphry's experience of India proved to be a bitter one, culminating in his sueing of the crew for lost earnings on his voyage home three years later when his cabin was too small for him to use as a studio.

Humphry had heard before he left England that Smart was planning to go to India as well. He was deeply anxious about such competition, and later further disquieted by the arrival of the 'pretty widow' miniaturist Mrs Hill (see Chapter 6). He thought of changing to oil, but the Governor warned him to stay with miniatures as originally agreed to 'avoid contention and jealousy'. In fact both Smart and Humphry suffered not from each other's presence but from difficulties in getting paid. The expatriate community certainly wanted their miniatures – there was much exchange of letters and miniatures on the mail ships that went back and forth. But unfortunately both Smart and Humphry found that the richest patrons, the Indian princes, while willing to employ an artist were less willing to pay them. One nawab owed Humphry for seven months work, but since he also owed the East India Company money their claim was put before that of Humphry. In contrast, Smart, a careful man, did relatively well in India. However, by the end of the eighteenth century the artistic community in London had learned that India was merely another market, with its own difficulties, and not a guarantee of fortune.

Opposite: Plate 70. Ozias Humphry, *Hyder Beg Khan* 1786. Watercolour on ivory (89 x 75 mm). Humphry was one of a number of miniaturists who travelled to India hoping to make their fortune. Evans 142

CHAPTER SIX

THE NINETEENTH CENTURY

Miniature as a Ladies' Pastime

By the end of the seventeenth century limning, which had earlier been practised as a gentlemanly amateur art, was increasingly thought to be more suited to ladies. At the time that Mrs Pepys famously took lessons in limning, John Aubrey, a friend of Samuel Cooper, wrote in an educational treatise that limning was 'too effeminate. Painting is more masculine and useful'.[1] Miniature painting became established as a ladylike pastime, benefiting some professional miniaturists who acted as drawing masters. One of Bernard Lens' many pupils was Catherina da Costa, daughter of a Jewish doctor from Portugal. Some of her miniature portraits of her family are now in the Jewish Museum, London. Da Costa also copied Old Masters, as did Sarah Stanley (daughter of Sir Hans Sloane) whose works dating from 1732–8 are now in the V&A.

As a genteel domestic pastime, miniature painting offered women with neither father nor husband to support them the chance to earn a respectable living, as in the case of Penelope Carwardine. In 1763 she appears, with two other women, among over 20 miniaturists listed in

Plate 71. Mrs Mee, formerly Miss Anna Foldsone, *Self-Portrait.* Watercolour on ivory (76 x 57 mm). Horace Walpole, writing to the Misses Berry when Miss Foldsone failed, again, to deliver their miniatures, noted: 'I have a solution of Miss Foldsone: she has a mother and eight brothers and sisters, who make her work incessantly to maintain them and who reckon it loss of time to them if she finishes any pictures that are paid for beforehand'. P.12-1962

Mortimer's Universal Director.[2] Interestingly, although these women were unmarried they were described as 'Mrs' – respectability was an important consideration at this time. A drawing by the satirist Thomas Rowlandson, of a gentleman sitting to a pretty female miniaturist, reverses the roles of painter and sitter as she averts her gaze and he stares lecherously at her.[3] The studio was an intimate setting and women were vulnerable to accusations of impropriety, even though sittings generally took place with the sitter's family and friends in attendance.

The diarist Joseph Farington noted that Mrs Mee's husband 'had consented to let her paint ladies only who were never to be attended by gentlemen' (Plate 71). Many women miniaturists chose (or were persuaded) not to work professionally after marriage. Miss Diana Dietz exhibited at the Royal Academy as a professional, but once married she exhibited as 'Mrs Hill (Hon. Exhib.)', indicating that she was classed as a genteel amateur. Widowed soon afterwards, she again took up painting professionally (until she remarried), adventurously travelling to India. Ozias Humphry recognised the threat to his practice from this 'pretty widow', commenting that he would 'rather have all the male painters in England landed in Bengal than this single woman'.

Towards the end of the eighteenth century miniature painting as an amateur art was further encouraged by the development of watercolour painting. Watercolour became the medium of the traveller, and painting in watercolour increased in popularity as a leisure activity.

Landscape watercolour 'drawing', like the older water-colour art of miniature painting, became a suitable accomplishment for girls.

Specialist shops opened to meet this interest (fig. 17), the most famous of which was Rudolf Ackermann's 'Repository of Arts'. Ackermann's business began in 1796 with a drawing academy on the Strand, expanding with the addition of a gallery of watercolours, many for sale; a circulating library of prints and drawings as teaching aids; a tea room; and a supply of drawing and painting materials for sale.[4] Even Charlotte Brontë's character of the poor governess, Jane Eyre, has materials to hand when she resolves to paint an imaginary portrait of the woman she believes her master must love in preference to her, telling herself 'take a piece of smooth ivory – you have one prepared in your drawing-box; take your palette, mix your freshest, finest, clearest tints; choose your most delicate camel-hair pencils; delineate carefully the loveliest face you can imagine'.

Miniature painting was, in part, considered appropriate for women because it was a delicate, clean and literally time-consuming art, and as a portrait art it was confined to the domestic sphere. In a letter to her nephew, Jane Austen drew an analogy between the narrow compass of miniature painting and the limited sphere of her own novels: 'What should I do with your strong, manly, spirited Sketches, full of Variety and Glow? – How could I possibly join them on to the little bit (two Inches wide) of Ivory on which I work with so fine a Brush, as produces little effect after much labour?'[5]

Most professional miniaturists, however, were men. A surprising number of these miniaturists attended the Royal Academy school as boys, gaining both technical skills from the life class and important social contacts to which girls did not have access. It is notable that most women miniaturists in the nineteenth century had male artists as relatives who introduced them to the professional world. Of the miniaturist Annie Dixon it has been written, 'she had no leisure…for acquiring academic

Figure 17. Anonymous, trade card for S. & I. Fuller, 1823. The 'Temple of Fancy' opened in 1809, one of a number of shops which sold materials to amateur artists. This trade card refers to 'Ivory paper', a mid-eighteenth century invention of pasteboard coated with plaster of Paris in gelatine, a cheap replacement for ivory. E.3494-1934

Plate 72. John Smart, *The Misses Harriet and Elizabeth Binney*, 1806.
Watercolour on paper (225 x 245 mm). To compete with the growing
number of watercolour artists, Smart began to work on paper.
This was less labour-intensive than ivory, allowing such large
'miniatures' to be produced cheaply. P.20-1978

rules...never copied a picture, nor studied from the antique...but, after all, taking an agreeable as well as faithful likeness, with delicacy in manipulation...[is] more essential for miniature painting than severe drawing or knowledge of rules'.[6] However, more women did want to train correctly and to practice with a view to gaining a reputation, not just a living. A review of Emma Kendrick's *Conversations on Miniature Painting* concluded that, for women, it was 'one of those "Royal Roads"...well adapted for young ladies who wish to amuse themselves with painting miniatures of their friends, as they would butterflies on rice paper; but it will never make an artist of them'.[7] Even though it was seen as an appropriate art form for women, any girl who aspired to paint miniatures for more than amusement had to take an altogether less certain route than her brothers.

The Status of Miniature Painting

By the nineteenth century, miniature painting was a popular and commercially successful art. However, since the seventeenth century, the artistic standing of miniatures had been open to question. As discussed previously, John Aubrey believed oils to be more 'masculine'; Ozias Humphry had believed it a 'disgrace' to be a miniaturist and, like Samuel Shelley, had developed techniques to emulate oils. Nonetheless, the Royal Academy had no official hierarchy of art, in contrast to the French Academy which designated miniature a lesser genre, and for most miniaturists the spur to change was not comparison with oil, but the daily realities of an overcrowded portrait market.

In the 1780s Cosway developed elegant full-length portrait drawings on paper, with the face finished in watercolour; at the end of the century John Smart began to paint larger watercolour portraits on paper (Plate 72). Such adaptations of traditional watercolour miniatures, in terms of size, format and base, occurred at a time when the younger technique of watercolour 'drawing' on paper was growing as an art form. Most watercolourists were landscape artists, but some began to specialise in figure watercolours, taking the logical step of entering the lucrative portraiture business. Miniaturists met the challenge in a variety of ways; as well as painting large watercolour portraits, Smart also developed small oval half-lengths on paper. These were less labour intensive than his usual miniatures, allowing him to compete with the quicker methods of working on paper.

Plate 73. Andrew Robertson, *Unknown Woman*, c.1825. Watercolour on ivory (81 x 67 mm). Robertson referred to oval miniatures such as those by Richard Cosway as 'baubles'. Although he developed a large rectangular format in a heavy watercolour that even Cosway thought was oil, Robertson was forced to paint 'ovals' to make a living. 23-1885

Most miniaturists were comfortable at the Royal Academy. Although the number of exhibits had increased dramatically from 139 in 1769 to 1194 by 1797, and watercolour drawings were squeezed into backrooms, miniature paintings remained at the heart of the main exhibition room (fig. 14). However, around 1805 a group of watercolourists decided to break with the Royal Academy. A letter was sent to leading miniature painters asking them to join in setting up a separate exhibiting society for watercolour.[8] The miniaturists, however, shared no fellow feeling with the watercolourists (most of whom were landscape artists), and did not feel disadvantaged at the Academy where most leading artists were portrait painters. Only Samuel Shelley joined, hoping that his commercially unsuccessful 'histories' would appear to better advantage when displayed away from the oils they emulated.

But if miniaturists felt that their place was among their

Plate 74. Alfred Edward Chalon, *Mrs. Peter de Wint*, wife of the landscape artist. Watercolour on ivory (103 x 83 mm). Robertson's heavily gummed manner imitating oil became the dominant style, but a few leading miniaturists such as Chalon worked in a lighter more sketchy fashion, leaving the ivory still apparent. P.43-1942

Opposite: Plate 75. William Charles Ross, *Mrs Bacon*, 1841. Watercolour on ivory (214 x 176 mm). Ross's miniatures often measured over a foot and a half, so at eight inches this is quite modest. P.68-1921

fellow portrait painters, they were soon to question this assumption. Soon after the opening of the Watercolour Society's first exhibition, Martin Archer Shee, a portrait painter in oil, an Academician and a future President of the Royal Academy, published an epic poem decrying the state of art in Britain. Shee's examination of the nation's failure to encourage advances in art effectively absolved artists from responsibility – with the exception of miniaturists. In an extraordinary attack on his fellow portrait artists he raged, 'Blockheads pursu'd through every nobler shape/in miniature take refuge and escape', and an extensive footnote elaborated the failings of miniaturists.[9]

The Academy had been set up to encourage art by training a new generation of painters in academic principles. But after a number of generations had been through the system, the public still preferred to commission portraits rather than encourage history painting. Portrait painters such as Shee could equally be blamed for pandering to this market, but Shee excused oil portraitists because they undertook academic study of the human figure. He argued that if the public chose to encourage history painting, the oil portraitists were trained to provide it. But miniature painters did not aspire to such heights; in his footnotes Shee explained his view that miniature painting was the choice of those who were too stupid and lazy to undertake academic study and wanted to make an easy living.

These were not abstract debates. Four years before Shee's outburst a young student, Andrew Robertson, joined the Academy School. Writing endless letters to his father in Scotland, he recorded the struggles which led him to develop a new style of miniature painting, which eventually set the standard for the next generation of miniaturists.[10] Robertson had earned his living as a miniaturist in Scotland and was anxious to establish his artistic reputation in London. He absorbed the lessons of the life class and raised his ambitions accordingly. Daring to show his earliest attempt at a miniature of a classical subject to the President of the Academy, Benjamin West, he was told that his work had 'none of the trifling insignificance of miniatures' and that its size 'was so large as to admit all the character' of portraiture in oil which could be lost in a small miniature. Robertson wrote to his father that 'oval miniatures…are, at best, but toys. I should like…to paint pictures', for 'most miniatures are too much like china', with their 'blueness and cold tone'. Robertson developed a 'great style' of miniature painting which emulated oil painting, and was delighted when fellow artists, especially Cosway,

Opposite: Plate 76. Alfred Tidey, *A Boy with White Mice, c.* 1845. Watercolour on ivory (193 x 137 mm). This is a rare example of a genre scene on ivory by an English miniaturist. It failed to sell when exhibited at the Royal Academy in 1845; as Tidey observed, the public only wanted portraits. P.85-1935

Figure 18. Francis Danby, detail of *Disappointed Love*, exhibited at the Royal Academy in 1821. Oil on panel (62.8 x 81.2 cm). Miniatures became symbols of love and affection with which others could empathise. In this simple narrative painting, a girl weeps with a discarded miniature and destroyed letters at her side.

mistook his new watercolour style for oil. When Robertson exhibited 'ovals' West was furious (Plate 73), but when he exhibited his 'new style' West rewarded him by giving his work a central position among the miniatures. Robertson absorbed the culture of the Academy and took to heart the opinions of those who sought to influence his work.

The 'New Style' of Miniature Painting

In some ways Robertson's innovations were not completely new. He increased the size of the ivory to allow for a more complicated composition, which Cotes (Plate 64) and Crosse (Plate 63) had both done. He used a rectangular shape rather than an oval, which Humphry had often used (Plate 70), and worked densely with a heavily gummed pigment much as Shelley had done (Plate 67). But Robertson combined these new elements, deliberately seeking to revolutionise the art, since he had quickly learned that the reputation of his branch of art was as a trifling, mercenary 'bauble'. This rather proved the point made by the miniaturist W. H. Watts in a published response to Shee's attack on miniaturists. He felt that the Society of Watercolour Painters should be seen as a symbol of independence from those who decided 'who can be admitted into the pale of respectability in the arts', namely the oil painters.[11] In fact watercolour artists were soon to pursue the same road as the miniaturists, with a more dense, finished style. One commentator noted wryly, 'Artists who give themselves so much trouble to do in water what they might easily do in oils are like romantic lovers who come in down the chimney when the door would be opened at the second knock'.[12]

In retrospect Robertson's innovations seem as inexplicable as the introduction of ivory as a base a hundred years earlier, in terms of the difficulty of the process and the labour required. For Robertson it also made little financial sense: 'Pictures of that large size take so much time to paint, that I should starve, were my employment altogether in these. They are what have gained me my reputation, but small miniatures are what one must live by' (Plate 73).

And yet a decade later Robertson attended an Academy exhibition and was struck by the fact that, 'with the exception of Chalon, those who distinguished themselves in miniature were more or less my pupils'. Robertson proudly added that Chalon had been advised by his tutor that 'this style would be followed and prevail, advising him at once to follow it' (Plate 74). Robertson's most successful pupil was Sir William Charles Ross, who began by helping Robertson with the backgrounds and drapery of his labour intensive miniatures. He later became miniature painter to Queen Victoria who knighted him in 1842. Ross's large miniatures, which sometimes measured over a foot and a half, were only affordable for a wealthy elite (Plate 75). Although his grand miniatures resembled the freedom of oil, the process was a hard-won effect achieved through meticulous repetitive touches. Ross's sister Mrs Dalton

Figure 19. John Field (1771–1848), *Silhouette of an Unknown Man*, ivory, set in a hair bracelet (32 x 21mm). The trade cards on the reverse of most larger 'profiles' (as they were called at this time) spell out their attractions: quick, conveniently reproducible and cheap. But as the fashion for profiles grew, more expensive variations developed, such as the work on ivory shown here. P.165-1922

Plate 77a and b. Charles Haytes, (a) *Unknown Woman and Two Children*, 1800; (b) *Unknown Boy*, holding the miniature to the right (both 89 x 71 mm). The boy's naval costume, popular as a school uniform, suggests that he is about to leave home. The presence of miniatures within a miniature portrait was a conceit which became more common at this time.
(a) P.23-1923; (b) P.24-1923

lived with him and helped him to paint, presumably fill-ing in the tedious backgrounds and draperies.[13]

Most miniaturists and sitters, however, lived far from the grand world in which Ross moved and consequently had very different expectations of miniature painting. Charles Dickens, whose aunt was a miniature painter, created a miniaturist character, Mrs la Creevy in *Nicholas Nickleby*, who became the epitome of the modest minia-turist providing a service rather than aspiring to paint great art. She was one of the many who from 'straitened circumstances, a consequent inability to form the associa-tion they would wish, and a disinclination to mix with the society they could obtain' found London to be 'as complete a solitude as the plains of Syria'. Dickens portrays the artist outside the professional and social intensity of the Royal Academy, lost in the mêlée of Victorian London, where people carved out small lives for themselves and just tried not to fall through the cracks.

Miniature Paintings in Nineteenth-Century Society

The proliferation of miniatures in the late eighteenth and early nineteenth centuries ensured a place for them in the emotional and social life of the day, reflected in literature and even in painting. Eighteenth- and nine-teenth-century novels employed the idea, first used by

Shakespeare, of the miniature as a symbol of intimacy and possession. In Jane Austen's *Persuasion,* a key discussion about love and fidelity is introduced by means of a miniature of a young man intended for his fiancée, who died before she could take possession of it. Having fallen in love again, the young man asks his greatest friend, his dead lover's brother, to get the minia-ture 'properly set for another', at which the brother exclaims 'Poor Fanny! she would not have forgotten him so soon!' In *Sense and Sensibility*, Eleanor's rival proves her prior claim to Edward Ferrars by producing his miniature from her pocket. Ozias Humphry pointed out the particular way in which the intimate size of the miniature, its ability to be carried on the person, made the symbolism of its ownership quite different from larger portraits. When Miss Boydell, his fiancée, broke off their engagement she returned Humphry's letters and his miniature and asked for the return of her letters and her miniature. Later Humphry gave this miniature of himself to his sister-in-law, saying bitterly that Miss Boydell had 'contaminated it'.

As seen earlier, Charlotte Brontë also employed minia-tures to make subtle points in *Jane Eyre*. Mrs Reed, the hard-hearted aunt of the young orphan Jane, locked her in a cold disused room which she herself only rarely visited 'to review the contents of a certain secret drawer in the wardrobe, where were stored divers parch-ments...and a miniature of her deceased husband'. On his death bed Mrs Reed's husband had charged her to look after Jane, but she had neglected her. Mr Reed's portrait miniature, which his wife could have carried at all times, is hidden away and seems akin to her conscience, which she only occasionally considers.

In George Eliot's *Middlemarch* Dorothea is shown around her betrothed's house, 'and there were minia-tures of ladies and gentlemen with powdered hair hanging in a group' – his mother's generation, painted when Cosway was the leading miniaturist and powdered hair was still the fashion. We think of small miniatures being worn by one owner or left in a jewellery box, but even small oval miniatures were displayed as we would today display a group of family photographs.

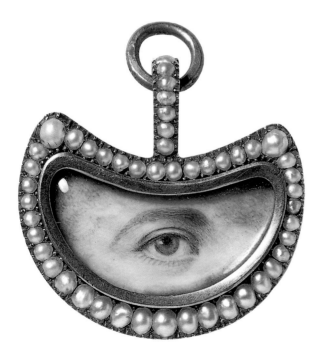

Fig. 20. Anonymous, early 19th century, crescent gold locket set with seed pearls (12 x 22mm). The brief vogue for eye miniatures was an example of one of miniature's stranger developments. P.55-1977

Plate 78a and b. (a) Charles Robertson (1760–1821), (64 x 51mm); (b) Mary Ann Knight (1766–1851), (60 x 48mm). Two portrait miniatures from the early 19th century showing the reverse set with hair ornaments. The gift of hair as a token was long-established and the back of a miniature provided a perfect dwelling for such 'relicks'.
(a) P.98-1962 and (b) P.41-1952

Plate 79 (actual size). William Edward Kilburn, hand-coloured daguerreotype of Maria Jane Wood, *c.*1850 (90 x 65 mm). Daguerreotype was one of the earliest photographic processes. The object was the original plate rather than a print, which was kept in a leather case similar to those used for miniatures. An oval miniature worn at the sitter's neck is a poignant presence within this new medium.

In the wake of the sentimentality attached to miniatures, other fashions came and went. In the late eighteenth century, the fashion for hair ornaments set in the back of miniature lockets developed (Plate 78). The giving of tokens of hair was a long-established practice. When Queen Charlotte appointed Samuel Finney as her miniature painter in 1763, she sent him a lock of her hair which, he wrote, should be 'preserved by his family with the same care and reverence as a good catholick would the relicks of his patron Saint'. The back of a miniature was a perfect setting for such tokens, but the fashion for hair ornaments grew to such an extent that they were sometimes merely decorative rather than sentimental.

Another fashion was the so-called 'eye miniature' which lasted a few decades from the end of the eighteenth century (fig. 20): 'A curious, brief but intense freak of the miniature art…aimed to capture the most intimate glance of "the windows of the soul" [but] more often captured a repulsively detailed, almost anatomical, account of the mere surface of the eye.'[14] No 'sitter' could ever be identified from so little information, and few of these tiny curiosities were signed.

The Advent of Photography and its Effect on the Miniature

In 1839 the new invention of photography first came to public notice. Within a decade, photography studios began to appear in London and by the late 1850s it was clear that photography was not a passing fad. The effect on miniature painting was both quick and surprising.

The Journal of the Photographic Society (1 September 1858) stated:

Amongst the many changes photography has produced in art...there is not, perhaps, a more striking instance to be found than that portion of the Royal Academy Exhibition called the Miniature Room. Time was when a whole side of that room was crowded, every nook and corner often spread out and occupying a large portion of each end...Photography has swept away very many third- or fourth-class miniature-painters, or turned them into photographic colourists – men who never ought to have adopted art as a profession. Nor do we any longer see cases at the private entrances of shops as formerly we did...[containing miniatures and informing the public that they could] *be done for a guinea on the first floor in the true Miss La Creevy style.*

The writer remembers how these miniaturists' cases reflected the clientele of the area: in Charing Cross, young men 'who had got into regimentals for the first time', in Aldgate Pump, clergymen, in Cheapside, naval men, and in Oxford Street, 'specimens of artistic ability' where the miniaturist painted his sitters dressed as Rubens or the Goddess Hebe. 'Where you were once "done" abominably for a guinea, you can be admirably taken for half the sum.' But the writer laments that such 'an inroad has been made in this branch of art, that it becomes a serious question whether we may not lose our miniature-painters entirely. A first-class miniature is, and must ever be, an expensive object, and those who can paint them are leaving the profession'.

The writer's assessment was correct. Thomas Carrick left the profession and set up a photography studio himself, as did a few other miniaturists. Techniques were even developed whereby ivory was coated with photographic emulsion and a faint likeness taken, which was then painted. It seemed the sun was a better artist in the eyes of most clients; even miniaturists who continued to work without the direct intervention of photography often showed a strong dependency on it. The miniaturist Alfred Tidey (1808–92) wrote in 1885 that efforts were being made to save this 'Art of the past', but that 'the great perfection to which photography has attained goes so far to satisfy the never ceasing and most cherished feelings of humanity and which the miniature painter alone could formerly supply (viz) likeness in little, that I fear it will be but a vain struggle'.[15] Miniature painting was supplanted in emotional and cultural life by photography. In a painting by John Everett Millais from 1871, *Yes or No* (Yale Center for British Art), the heroine does not hold a miniature of her lover but a carte de visite, a small photograph on a card.[16]

As soon as miniature painting ceased to be a vibrant contemporary practice, it became established as an aspect of British artistic history and a new place was carved out for it as a cultural artefact. The South Kensington Museum (now the V&A) was established in 1857, and in 1865 it held a huge exhibition of miniatures. In the introduction to the catalogue the Director wrote: 'We trust it is not beyond hope that the Exhibition of the works of so many distinguished men, and the beauty of their art, may lead to its revival'. Perhaps aware that this was a vain hope, he added that it was not unreasonable to expect that the exhibition would lead to 'a more general appreciation of the value of the works which remain to us, and tend to their better preservation; for it is truly painful to see how many fine miniatures have...suffered...from the absence of the most ordinary protection required for works of such minute delicacy'.[17]

Queen Victoria, under the watchful eye of her beloved Albert, had already undertaken the care of the Royal Collection of miniatures. They were gathered up from disparate hiding places and, 'excepting those of Albert and the Children, which I always have with me', reframed and catalogued. As she wrote in her diary, 'I know they are safe and cannot be lost whereas if they were carried about in boxes or left in drawers they were forgotten and might be lost and injured'.[18]

The care of the families to whom these intimate objects belonged has ensured that many have survived. The establishment of the South Kensington Museum at the very moment that miniature painting went into decline, and its early efforts at reappraisal of the art, made it a focus for interest in miniatures. The V&A collection initially grew not through purchases but through gifts from the children and grandchildren of artists or from the descendants of sitters – as Queen Victoria commented of her own collection, 'All for futurity and for the general good'.

NOTES

PRIMARY SOURCES

The following primary sources have been used extensively throughout the text, referred to by author, with only one footnote when first mentioned.

Buckeridge, Bainbrigge, in de Piles' *The Art of Painting and the Lives of the Painters* (translated into English, 1706).

Finney, Samuel – I am indebted to R.B. Delderfield for generously allowing me to use freely his transcript of Samuel Finney's papers held by the Cheshire Record Office.

Graham, Richard, in du Fresnoy's *Art of Painting* (translated into English by Mr Dryden, 1695).

Haydocke, Richard *A Tracte containing the Artes of Curious Paintings, Carvings & Buildings* (translation of G.P. Lomazzo's *Trattato dell'arte de la pittura*, Oxford 1598).

Nicholas Hilliard 'A Treatise Concerning the Arte of Limning', MS.Laing III, 174, Edinburgh University; ed. R.K.R. Thornton and T.G.S. Cain as *The Arte of Limning* (Mid-Northumberland Arts Group, 1981).

Humphrey, Ozias. See J.Agnew's *Report on the Papers of Ozias Humphry, RA (1743–1810) in the Custody of the Royal Academy of Arts* (Royal Commission on Historical Manuscripts, 1972).

Norgate, Edward Bodleian Library MS. Tann 326; ed. Martin Hardie as *Miniatura or the Art of Limning* (Oxford, 1919).

Robertson, Andrew *Letters and Papers of Andrew Robertson* (E.Robertson ed., 1879).

Vertue, George 'Note Books I–VI', *Walpole Society* (1929–30/1951-2), vols XVIII/XXX.

DICTIONARIES

Foskett, Daphne *A Dictionary of British Miniature Painters*, 2 vols (1972).

Long, Basil *British Miniaturists* (1929).

Schidlof, Leo R. *The Miniature in Europe*, 4 vols (Akademische Druck-U. Verlagsanstalt, Graz-Austria, 1964).

Introduction

1 See Primary Sources: Haydocke, Richard.

2 See Primary Sources: Norgate, Edward.

3 Edmond, Mary *Hilliard and Oliver; the Lives and Works of Two Great Miniaturists* (London, 1983), p.77.

4 Quoted by Piper, David *The English Face* (Thames and Hudson, 1957), p.124.

5 See Primary Sources: Graham, Richard.

6 See Primary Sources: Buckeridge, Bainbrigge.

7 See Primary Sources: Vertue, George.

8 South Kensington Museum Catalogue, *Exhibition of Portrait Miniatures* (1865), p.iv.

Chapter 1

1 Quoted by Auerbach, Erna *Nicholas Hilliard* (Routledge and Kegan Paul, London, 1961), p.45.

2 Society of Antiquaries Manuscript 129, to be published by Harvey Miller, edited by David Starkey, *Inventory of Henry VIII, Volume I, the Transcript* (forthcoming, 1997).

3 C. Winter, noted by Murrell, Jim *The Way Howe to Lymne; Tudor Miniatures Observed* (Victoria and Albert Museum, 1983), p.4.

4 Mander III, Karel van *Schilderboek* (1604); translated into English by Constant van der Wall (New York 1936), p.89.

5 Paget, Hugh 'Gerard and Lucas Hornebolte in England', *Burlington Magazine* (November 1959), vol CI, pp.396–402.

6 G.Reynolds, noted by Murrell, Jim *The Way Howe to Lymne; Tudor Miniatures Observed* (Victoria and Albert Museum, 1983), p.5, n.10.

7 Lorne Campbell and Susan Foister provide an expanded discussion of the known facts about the Horneboltes in 'Gerard, Lucas and Susannah Horenbout', *Burlington Magazine* (1986), no.128, p.719–727.

8 T.H. Colding, noted by Murrell, Jim *The Way Howe to Lymne; Tudor Miniatures Observed* (Victoria and Albert Museum, 1983), p.5.

9 Murrell, Jim *The Way Howe to Lymne; Tudor Miniatures Observed* (Victoria and Albert Museum, 1983), pp.5–12.

10 ibid p.23.

11 For discussion of the origins of the portrait miniature see Colding, T.H. *Aspects of Miniature Painting* (Copenhagen 1953); Backhouse, J. 'Illustrated Manuscripts and the Early Development of the Portrait Miniature in Early Tudor England', *Proceedings of the 1987 Harlaxton Symposium*, edited by Daniel Williams, (The Boydell Press, 1989); Backhouse, J. 'Illuminated Manuscripts and the Development of the Portrait Miniature' in Starkey, David, ed. *Henry VIII, A European Court in England* (Collins and Brown in association with the National Maritime Museum, Greenwich, 1991).

12 Quoted in Strong, Roy *The English Renaissance Miniature* (Thames and Hudson, 1983), pp.27–8.

13 Mellen, Peter *Jean Clouet; Complete Edition of the Drawings, Miniatures and Paintings* (Phaidon, 1971, p.10).

14 *Artists of the Tudor Court, the Portrait Miniature Rediscovered 1520–1620* (Victoria and Albert Museum exhibition 1983), Roy Strong with contributions from V. J. Murrell, p.9.

15 Strong *Renaissance Miniature* op.cit. p.28. It was the suggestion of John Burnett, formerly of the Science Museum, that a 'spechi da fuoco' may have been a burning glass.

16 Auerbach, Erna *Tudor Artists* (University of London, the Athlone Press, 1954), pp. 68–9.

17 ibid p.69.

18 Noted by C. Lloyd and V. Remington *Masterpieces in Little, Portrait Miniatures from the Collection of Her Majesty Queen Elizabeth II* (Royal Collection Enterprises Limited 1997), p.12.

19 *Artists of the Tudor Court* op.cit., cat. no. 13.

20 Foister, Susan 'Holbein as Court Painter' in Starkey ed. *Henry VIII* op.cit., p.62.

21 Campbell, Lorne 'Holbein's Miniature of "Mrs Pemberton": The Identity of the Sitter', *Burlington Magazine* (1987), vol CXXIX pp.366–371.

22 Quoted by Foister, Susan 'Holbein as Court Painter' in Starkey ed. *Henry VIII* op.cit., p.61.

23 Murrell *Way Howe to Lymne* op.cit., pp.9–12.

24 ibid p.12.

25 Lloyd and Remington *Masterpieces in Little* op.cit., p.12.

26 Strong *Renaissance Miniature* op.cit. pp.54–64.

27 See, for example, G. Reynolds 'The English Miniature of the Renaissance: A "Rediscovery" Examined', *Apollo* (1983), vol CXVIII, pp.308–311; and S. Foister 'Exhibition Review; Tudor Minaturists at the V&A', *Burlington Magazine* (1983), vol CXXV, p.635.

28 For discussion of Shute and Bettes, see Strong *Renaissance Miniature* op.cit., pp.56–7.

29 Strong *Renaissance Miniature* op.cit. pp.7–9.

Chapter 2

1 Edmond *Hilliard and Oliver* op.cit., p.29.

2 Murrell *Way Howe to Lymne* op.cit. illustrated Plate 45, discussed p.28–9.

3 Harley, R.D. *Artist's Pigments c1600–1835* (Butterworth Scientific, second edition 1982), p.5.

4 Murrell *Way Howe to Lymne* op.cit., p.13.

5 Bimbenet-Privat, Michele *Les Orfevres Parisiens de la Renaissance (1506–1620)* (Commission des travaux historiques de la ville de Paris 1992), p.504. I am grateful to Philippa Glanville for informing me of this reference to 'Nicholas Heliart (compagnon anglais) 16 November, 1578'.

6 *Artists of the Tudor Court* op.cit., cat. nos. 185 and 186. For discussion of Plate 12, 'Robert Dudley'(now in the V&A, E.1174-1988), see Roy Strong 'The Leicester House Miniatures: Robert Sidney, Ist Earl of Leicester and his Circle', *Burlington Magazine* (October 1985), p.694.

7 Lloyd and Remington *Masterpieces in Little* op.cit., p.12.

8 Edmond *Hilliard and Oliver* op.cit., p.65.

9 *Artists of the Tudor Court* op.cit., p.13.

10 MacTaggart, Peter and Anne 'The Rich Wearing Apparel of Richard, 3rd Earl of Dorset', *Costume* (1980), vol XIV, pp.41–55. Quoted in *Artists of the Tudor Court* op.cit., cat.no. 276.

11 William Camden (1605), quoted by Edmond *Hilliard and Oliver* op.cit., p.87.

12 *Artists of the Tudor Court* op.cit. cat. no. 136.

13 Quoted in Strong, Roy *Henry Prince of Wales and England's Lost Renaissance* (Thames and Hudson, 1986), p.49.

14 *Artists of the Tudor Court* op.cit. cat. no. 179.

15 Noted by Reynolds, Graham *Nicholas Hilliard and Isaac Oliver* (London, Her Majesty's Stationery Office, 1971), p.19.

16 *Princely Magnificence, Court Jewels of the Renaissance, 1500–1630* (Debrett's Peerage Limited, in association with the Victoria and Albert Museum, 1980), illustrated cat. no. P15.

Chapter 3

1 Quoted in Edmond *Hilliard and Oliver* op.cit., p.142.

2 Reynolds, Graham 'Portraits by Nicholas Hilliard and his Assistants of King James I and his Family', *The Walpole Society* (1952–4) vol. XXXIV, pp.14–26.

3 ibid.

4 Strong *Henry Prince of Wales* op.cit. pp.117–8. For further discussion of Oliver as a possible oil painter see Edmond *Hilliard and Oliver* op.cit., pp.153–4.

5 *Artists of the Tudor Court* op.cit., see under cat.no.181.

6 Edmond *Hilliard and Oliver* op.cit., illustrated Plate 30.

7 Murdoch, John *Seventeenth-Century English Miniatures in the Collection of the Victoria and Albert Museum* (The Stationery Office, 1997). See biography of Gerbier.

8 Reynolds, Graham 'A Newly Identified Miniaturist of the Early Seventeeth Century' *Burlington Magazine* (July 1949), vol XCI, pp.196–7.

9 Quoted by Girouard, M. *Life in the English Country House* (Penguin Books, 1980), p.172.

10 Quoted by Talley, M.K. *Portrait Painting in England; Studies in the Technical Literature before 1700* (Guildford, 1981), p.70.

11 ibid p.65.

12 Murdoch *Seventeenth Century English Miniatures* op.cit. See under catalogue entry for Peter Oliver, 'Tarquin and Lucretia' (1787–1869).

13 Quoted by Edmond *Hilliard and Oliver* op.cit., pp.72–3.

14 ibid p. 72.

15 Edmond, Mary 'Limners and Picturemakers: New Light on the Lives of the Miniaturists and Large-Scale Portrait-Painters working in London in the Sixteenth and Seventeeenth Centuries', *Walpole Society* (1978–80), vol. XLVII, p.96.

16 Edmond 'Limners and Picturemakers' op.cit., p.69.

17 Murdoch *Seventeenth-Century English Miniatures* op.cit. See under biography of Hoskins.

18 Reynolds, Graham *English Portrait Miniatures, Revised Edition* (Cambridge University Press 1988) p.38.

19 Edmond 'Limners and Picturemakers' op.cit. p.64.

20 Edmond *Hilliard and Oliver* op.cit., p.170.

21 Edmond 'Limners and Picturemakers' op.cit., p.97.

22 ibid p.99.

23 J. von Sandrart *Academia Noblissimae Artis Pictoriae* (1683), p.312.

24 Murdoch *Seventeenth-Century English Miniatures* op.cit. See under biography of Gerbier.

25 *Artists of the Tudor Court* op.cit. See under cat. no.181.

26 Murdoch *Seventeenth-Century English Miniatures* op.cit. See under catalogue entry for Peter Oliver, 'Tarquin and Lucretia' (1787–1869).

27 Edmond 'Limners and Picturemakers' op.cit., p.125.

28 Quoted by D. Piper *The English Face* (Thames and Hudson 1957), p.124.

29 Murdoch *Seventeenth-Century English Miniatures* op.cit., see under catalogue entry for Peter Oliver 'A girl, believed to be Venetia Stanley, Lady Digby' (P.3-1950).

Chapter 4

1 Foskett, Daphne *Samuel Cooper 1609–1672* (Faber & Faber 1974), p.34.

2 Edmond 'Limners and Picturemakers' op.cit., p.102.

3 ibid pp.70–1.

4 Goulding, R. W. 'The Welbeck Abbey Minatures', *Walpole Society* (1916) vol. IV, pp.29–30.

5 Edmond 'Limners and Picturemakers' op.cit., p.102.

6 ibid pp.105–6.

7 Murdoch *Seventeenth-Century English Miniatures* op.cit., quoted under biography of Gibson.

8 Gibson, Katharine, forthcoming PhD, 'The Iconography of Charles II', Courtauld Institute, University of London, in which she details discoveries made in the Royal Household lists pertaining to artists' appointments at Court.

9 Porter, Roy *London, A Social History* (Penguin Books 1996), p.131.

10 Murdoch, Murrell, Noon and Strong *The English Miniature* (Yale University Press 1981); Murrell p.15.

11 ibid; Murdoch pp.151–3.

12 Murdoch *Seventeenth-Century English Miniatures* op.cit., see under catalogue entry for Thomas Flatman 'An unknown Woman, perhaps Alice Beale' (P.14-1941).

13 Murdoch, Murrell, Noon and Strong *The English Miniature* op.cit.; Murdoch pp.155–6.

14 Reynolds, Graham *Samuel Cooper's Pocket Book* (Victoria and Albert Museum Brochure 8, 1975).

15 Bignamini, Ilaria 'Art Institutions in London, 1689–1768: A Study of Clubs and Academies', *The Walpole Society* (1988) vol. LIV pp.22–44.

16 Walker, Richard *Miniatures in the Collection of Her Majesty the Queen. The Eighteenth and Early Nineteenth Centuries* (Cambridge University Press 1992), cat. no. 126.

17 Murdoch, Murrell, Noon and Strong *The English Miniature* op.cit.; Noon, illustrated fig.188.

18 *The Complete Edition of the Oxford English Dictionary* (Book Club Associates, London 1979).

19 ibid.

20 Walker *Miniatures in the Collection of Her Majesty the Queen. The Eighteenth and Early Nineteenth Centuries* op.cit., p.xiv.

21 Bignamini, Ilaria 'The Accompaniement to Patronage. A study of the origins, rise and development of an institutional system for the arts in Britain, 1692–1768'. Unpublished PhD thesis (Courtauld Institute of Art, University of London, 1988).

22 Goulding *The Welbeck Abbey Miniatures* op.cit., p.41.

23 Christie's sale *Important English and Continental Miniatures* (Tuesday, November 2, 1971), illustrated cat. nos. 115–129.

24 Bignamini 'Art Institutions in London' op.cit., p.45 and note 14.

Chapter 5

1 Reynolds, Graham *English Portrait Miniatures* (London 1952), p.120.

2 For fuller discussion of the development of techniques at this date see Murdoch, Murrell, Noon and Strong *The English Miniature* op.cit.; Murrell pp.16–24.

3 ibid p.21, and see Long, Basil 'Miniaturists, their Desks and Boxes', *Connoisseur* (1929) vol. LXXXIII, pp.323–7.

4 See Primary Sources: Finney, Samuel.

5 For discussion of the development of life drawing in England see I. Bignamini and M. Postle *The Artist's Model, its Role in British Art from Lely to Etty* (Nottingham University Art Gallery 1991).

6 Lloyd, Stephen *Richard and Maria Cosway, Regency Artists of Taste and Fashion* (The National Galleries of Scotland 1995), p.22.

7 D. Hudson and K.W. Luckhurst, *The Royal Society of Arts (1754–1954)*, (John Murray 1954), p.8.

8 See Primary Sources: Humphry, Ozias.

9 Quoted by Lloyd *Cosway* op.cit., p.23.

10 Hudson and Luckhurst *Royal Society of Arts* op.cit., p.35.

11 ibid p.37

12 Walker *Miniatures in the Collection of Her Majesty the Queen. The Eighteenth and Early Nineteenth Centuries* op.cit., cat. no. 234, p.xiv, Humphrey, cat. no. 234.

13 For the identity of this sitter see Lloyd *Cosway* op.cit., cat. no.16.

14 For further discussion of miniature painting in the provinces see Foskett, Daphne *Collecting Miniatures* (The Antique Collectors' Club 1979), chapter VIII.

15 Plumb, J. H. *England in the Eighteenth Century* (Penguin Books, reprinted 1981), p.174.

Chapter 6

1 Quoted by Wendorf, Richard *The Elements of Life, Biography and Portrait-Painting in Stuart and Georgian England* (Clarendon Press 1990), p.122.

2 Reynolds *English Portrait Miniatures* (1952) op.cit. p.131.

3 Illustrated in Pointon, Marcia *Hanging the Head: Portraiture and social formation in eighteenth-century England* (Yale University Press 1993), Plate 61.

4 J. Krill *English Artists' Paper* (Trefoil 1987), pp.111–113.

5 Quoted by Fiona Stafford in an Introduction to Jane Austen's *Emma* (Penguin Classics 1996).

6 Clayton, Ellen *English Female Artists* (1876), p.252.

7 Review of Emma E. Kendrick *Conversations on the Art of Miniature Painting* (1830), from *The Library of the Fine Arts* (1831) vol. I, pp.245–266.

8 Roget, J. L. *A History of the 'Old Watercolour Society'* (1891), p.132.

9 Shee, Martin Archer *Rhymes on Art, or the Remonstrance of a Painter* (1805), pp.30–31.

10 See Primary Sources: Robertson, Andrew.

11 Watts, W. H. *The Remonstrancer Remonstrated With* (1806).

12 Murdoch, Murrell, Noon and Strong *The English Miniature* op.cit.; quoted by Noon p.207.

13 Clayton *English Female Artists* op.cit., p.254.

14 Piper *The English Face* op.cit., p.243.

15 Attached to the reverse of Tidey's 'A Boy with White Mice' (P.85-1935) and quoted in full in Murdoch, Murrell, Noon and Strong *The English Miniature* op.cit. p.223, note 59.

16 ibid p.209.

17 South Kensington Museum Catalogue: *Exhibition of Portrait Miniatures* (1865), p.xii.

18 Walker *Miniatures in the Collection of Her Majesty the Queen. The Eighteenth and Early Nineteenth Centuries* op.cit., pp. xxii–xxiii.

Miniatures Timeline

Artists illustrated	Relevant arts events in England	Relevant historical events	Reigns
	1500		
Lucas Hornebolte (c.1490/5 – 1544)	c.1526: First miniature painted at the court of Henry VIII 1526: Holbein visits England 1532: Holbein comes to England a second time, works for Henry VIII	1516: birth of Princess Mary, daughter of Catherine of Aragon 1533: birth of Princess Elizabeth, daughter of Anne Boleyn 1534: Henry breaks with Catholic church of Rome, and is pronounced Supreme Head of the Church of England 1537: birth of Prince Edward, son of Jane Seymour 1540: Henry marries Anne of Cleves	Henry VIII (1509–1647)
Levina Teerlinc (1510/20 – 1576)	1539: Holbein paints Anne of Cleves 1545 (?): Teerlinc appointed 'Paintrix' by Henry VIII		Edward VI (1547–53)
	1550		
		1553: Plot to make Lady Jane Gray queen in place of the Catholic Mary fails. Lady Jane is executed	
		Persecution of Protestants	Mary I (1553–8)
Nicholas Hilliard (c.1547–1619) Isaac Oliver (c.1560–1617)	1572: Elizabeth I's first sitting with Hilliard 1576–8: Hilliard in France 1587: Earliest known portrait miniature by Isaac Oliver 1596: John Donne's poem *Elegie: His Picture* pays tribute to the miniature as a parting gift between lovers 1598: Richard Haydocke publishes *A Tracte containing the Artes of Curious Paintings, Carvings & Buildings* c.1598: Hilliard writes 'A Treatise Concerning the Arte of Limning'; much plagarised later	1568: Mary Queen of Scots begins 19 years in the custody of Elizabeth I 1587: Mary is executed 1588: Catholic Spain sends Armada to England; defeated by the English fleet led by Sir Francis Drake 1596: birth of Princess Elizabeth; became Queen Elizabeth of Bohemia in 1620, and was grandmother of the future George I	Elizabeth I (1558–1603

1600

Sir James Palmer (1584–1657)	c.1600: In Shakespeare's Twelfth Night Olivia gives to Viola, whom she believes to be a man, a miniature as token of her love	1612: Prince Henry, Prince of Wales, dies. His brother Charles becomes Prince of Wales	James I (1603–25)
	1603: Hilliard remains limner to the crown		
	1605: Oliver appointed limner to the new Queen, Anne of Denmark		
Balthazar Gerbier (1592–1667)	1616: Gerbier comes to England		
John Hoskins (c.1590–1664/5)	Early 1620s: Hoskins takes on his nephew, Samuel Cooper		Charles I (1625–49)
	1632: Van Dyck comes to England at the invitation of Charles I		
	1637: Jean Petitot introduces the court of Charles I to enamel painting		
Samuel Cooper (1608–72)	1642: Cooper sets up independently of his uncle, in London	1642–49: Civil War – King against Parliament	
		1649: Charles I executed. Rule by Parliament dominated by the army	Interregnum (1649–60)

1650

Richard Gibson (?1605–1690)	c.1650–60: Plumbago introduced to England	1653–58: Oliver Cromwell acts as 'Lord Protector'	
Nicholas Dixon (fl.c.1660–1708)	1660: Cooper becomes king's limner	1660: Restoration of the monarchy. Charles II invited back from exile	Charles II (1660–85)
	1660: Samuel Pepys begins his famous diary of life in London during reign of Charles II		
	1660: Gibson sets up as professional limner in London		
Peter Cross (c.1645–1724)			
Thomas Flatman (1635–1688)			
Susannah Penelope Rosse (c.1652–1700)			
Charles Beale, junior (1660–1714)	Sir Peter Lely (1618–80) is the leading oil portraitist for Charles II. Several limners, including Beale, study in his studio		James II (1685–8)
		1688: 'The Glorious Revolution'. Mary, daughter of Charles II, and her husband William, Prince of Orange, depose her uncle, the Catholic James II	William II (1688–1702) and Mary II (1688–94)
	1689: First meeting of England's first artists' club, the 'Virtuosi of St Luke'		

1700

	Early 18th century: Grand Tour gains popularity		Anne (1702–14)
	1704: New artists' club founded, the 'Rose and Crown'		
	1705: Venetian artist Rosalba Carriera submits miniature on new base of ivory as her diploma piece to Rome's Academy of St Luke		

Bernard Lens III (1682–1740)	1707: Lens paints first miniature on ivory known in England 1711: Founding of Sir Godfrey Knellers's Academy of Drawing 1717: George Vertue made official engraver to the Society of Antiquaries, collects information about the history of art in Britain	1714: Anne dies without an heir. George, Protestant Elector of Hanover and grandson of Elizabeth of Bohemia, is invited to the British throne	George I (1714–27)
Samuel Finney (1718–98) Gervase Spencer (? –1763)		1721–42: Robert Walpole, father of Horace, in office as Britain's first Prime Minister	George II (1727–60)

1750

Nathanial Hone (1718–1784) Luke Sullivan (1705–1771) Jeremiah Meyer (1735–1789)	1753: British Museum established by Sir Hans Soane 1760: Founding of the Society of Artists. At the first exhibition, exhibitors include Finney, Hone, Meyer, Crosse, Cosway, Cotes 1762–71: Publication of Horace Walpole's *Anecdotes of Painting in England*, based on his purchase of Vertue's notes	1756–63: Seven Years War. European war, including concerns in Canada and India	George III (1760–1820)
Richard Crosse (1742–1810) Richard Cosway (1742–1821)	1763: Finney is appointed Miniature Painter to Queen Charlotte 1765: Society of Artists of Ireland holds first exhibition 1768: Founding of the Royal Academy. Founder members include Hone and Meyer; Joshua Reynolds is first President 1769: First RA summer exhibition; Cotes is one of the first exhibitors	From 1763: The East India Company (trading concern) acts increasingly as England's representative in India	
John Smart (1742–1811)	1778: Smart becomes President of Society of Artists 1785–95: Smart works in India	1776: American War of Independence	
Ozias Humphry (1742–1810) Samuel Cotes (1734–1818) Samuel Shelley (1750/56–1808) Thomas Hazelhurst (*c.*1740–*c.*1821)	1785–87: Humphrey works in India 1796: Randolph Ackermann opens drawing academy 1798: Ackermann re–names his business the Repository of Arts, serving the growing interest in watercolour as an amateur art Late 18th century: eye miniatures briefly in vogue	1783: French Revolution 1797: Beginning of the Napoleonic War	

1800

Charles Hayter (1761–1835)	*c.*1770–*c.*1850: Silhouettes established commercially as a rival art form of small portraiture (known as 'profiles') 1805: First exhibition of the new Society of Watercolour Painters. Shelley is a founder member	1805: Nelson's victory against Napoleon at Trafalgar

Mrs Mee, née Anna Foldsone (c.1770/5–1851)
Andrew Robertson (1777–1845)
Alfred Edward Chalon (1780–1860)
Sir William Charles Ross (1794/5–1860)
Alfred Tidey (1808–92)

1811 and 1815: Miniatures feature as key narrative elements in both Austen's *Sense and Sensibility* and *Persuasion*

1838–9: Dickens features an impoverished woman miniature painter in *Nicholas Nickleby*
1839: invention of photography; firmly established by 1850s
1842: Ross becomes Academician and is knighted by Queen Victoria
1847: Charlotte Bronte's *Jane Eyre*, set in the early 1800s, uses a miniature as a narrative device

1815: Wellington's victory against Napoleon at Waterloo

George IV (1820–30)

William IV (1830–37)

Victoria (1837–1901)

1850

1857: Foundation of the V&A (as the South Kensington Museum)
1858: *Journal of the Photographic Society* warns of threat of photography to miniature painting
1865: South Kensington Museum holds exhibition of 4000 miniatures

1861: Prince Albert, the Prince Consort, dies

INDEX